STRUCTURE AS ARCHITECTURE

STRUCTURE AS ARCHITECTURE

A SOURCE BOOK FOR ARCHITECTS AND STRUCTURAL ENGINEERS

Andrew W. Charleson

ELSEVIER

AMSTERDAM • BOSTON • HEIDELBERG • LONDON • NEW YORK • OXFORD
PARIS • SAN DIEGO • SAN FRANCISCO • SINGAPORE • SYDNEY • TOKYO
Architectural Press is an imprint of Elsevier

Architectural
Press

An imprint of Elsevier
Linacre House, Jordan Hill, Oxford OX2 8DP
30 Corporate Drive, Burlington MA 01803

First published 2005

British Library Cataloguing in Publication Data
A catalogue record for this book is available from the British Library

Library of Congress Cataloguing in Publication Data
A catalogue record for this book is available from the Library of Congress

ISBN 0 7506 6527 0

For information on all Architectural Press publications
visit our website at www.architecturalpress.com

Typeset by Charon Tec Pvt. Ltd, Chennai, India
www.charontec.com
Printed and bound in Italy

CONTENTS

PREFACE

This book explores the potential of structure, that is beams, columns, frames, struts and other structural members, to enrich architecture. At the most basic level I hope to raise architects' perception of structure as an integral element of architecture rather than as just an applied technology. I also wish to challenge architects to design structure themselves. That is, to attend to all aspects of its design, in collaboration with structural engineers of course, in order to realize their design concepts. Where structure contributes architecturally, other than in its primary load-bearing role, it contributes another layer of aesthetic and functional richness to designs. It increases interest in and enjoyment of buildings, improves their usability, and raises the spirits of their occupants.

This book therefore seeks to change a view of structure, common among architectural students at least, as a purely technical component of architecture, and at worst, a necessary evil. Examples throughout the book illustrate structure as an indispensable architectural element that is thoroughly integrated and involved in the making of architecture, and playing significant roles that engage the senses, hearts and minds of building users. As designers, we need to ask ourselves how structure might assist us to add aesthetic and functional value to our design work, thereby enriching it.

I write primarily for architectural students and practising architects, but expect the book will be of more than passing interest to engineering students and structural engineers who also wish to expand their awareness of the architectural potential of structure. The book, illustrated with examples from more than one hundred and seventy buildings, is intended to function both as a source book for architectural design inspiration and ideas, and as a book to assist designers to reflect upon their own work. It provides a large resource of very diverse precedents where structure enhances specific architectural ideas, concepts and qualities. The index collates these issues and an alphabetical list of all the case studies discussed provides initial references for further study.

The initial research from which this book has developed began as a literature review. However, limitations in this approach became apparent. Books for architectural students about structures tend to concentrate on the mechanics of structural analysis and design, and rarely explore the architectural implications of structure. Architectural design texts are also of limited value for this exercise. They certainly describe and analyse the elements of architecture, including structure, but apart from examining structure's space-defining and ordering roles, they throw little light on other areas where structure contributes architecturally. Also, many of their case studies draw upon pre-twentieth-century masonry buildings, rather than upon buildings incorporating modern structural materials and systems. Unfortunately, attempts to analyse structures' architectural contributions to selected buildings from more general architectural literature also proved relatively unsuccessful. Due to insufficient written and visual material related specifically to building structures, too many questions about their non-structural roles remained unanswered. Published photographic images usually provide very limited and selective views of a building and are a poor substitute for visiting it.

The alternative approach was to undertake field trips, so during the more intensive periods of research in 1993, 2001 and 2004 I visited, studied and analysed over two hundred and fifty mainly contemporary buildings. Most were selected before travelling after visually scanning many architectural books and periodicals published during the previous five to ten years. The key selection criterion was the degree to which their structures contribute architecturally, rather than any other architectural or structural design features. Where practicable, the second and third field trip itineraries included 'iconic' buildings as reviewed in Thiel-Siling, S. (ed.) (1998) *Icons of Architecture: The 20th Century* (Prestel). I approached the chosen buildings as open as possible to any architectural enrichment their structures might provide. A checklist helped focus observations and concentration, particularly when activities and displays in and around a building were more engaging than the structure itself!

By the term *analysed* I do not refer to quantitative analysis, practised daily by structural engineers, but rather to a qualitative analytical process comprising observation and focused reflection – the aim being to deepen an understanding and appreciation of structural and architectural interactions. Such an analytical process necessitates subjective readings of structure which inevitably emanate from my thirty years' experience as a structural engineer, the last eighteen of which have been spent teaching Structures in a school of architecture.

The scope of the book is limited geographically and by building typology. Not only do my school's library holdings privilege Western architecture, but the buildings that were selected as worth studying and could be included in realistic itineraries are located mainly within Western Europe, and to a more limited extent in North America. Regarding building typology, domestic dwellings are excluded from the study due to difficulties accessing them and there being no lack of more public alternatives. A wide range of building sizes is included, but no emphasis is placed on heroic long-span or high-rise structures whose scale can limit their relevance as precedents for the more modestly scaled designs undertaken by architectural students and most architects. Concern for the buildings' relevance to readers has also led to a concentration on contemporary buildings, with most completed during or since the 1990s.

Andrew W. Charleson

ACKNOWLEDGEMENTS

Various organizations have provided financial support for this project. The Cement and Concrete Association of New Zealand, the Steel Construction Industry of New Zealand, the New Zealand Timber Design Society and Victoria University of Wellington contributed towards the first field-study costs in 1992. Their generosity, repeated for a second trip in 2001, was supplemented by university summer research grants before, between and after those trips. Victoria University also funded the final field study to the USA in 2004.

I am most grateful for several research assistants who have brought much to this work. Jim McKie and Virginia Jamieson were involved at that delicate stage when the research was in its infancy and they were followed by Greg Miller who assisted with the preparatory work for the 2001 study trip. Sam Martin and Katherine Bowron continued when the book was taking shape, bringing the perspectives of senior architectural students to bear on the chapter drafts. Katherine produced the diagrams.

Numerous colleagues in the Schools of Architecture and Design have made helpful contributions. Comments from Mark Taylor, Julieanna Preston, Martin Hanley, Anna Kemble Welch, Christina McKay, Elizabeth and Peter Russell, Geoff Thomas, Robin Skinner and George Baird have helped improve and resolve the first two chapters, particularly in their early stages. The advice of John Gray and Werner Osterhaus, and the assistance of the Schools of Architecture and Design library staff has also been greatly appreciated. Paul Hillier and Ella Reed of the photographic section have worked with hundreds of images while Peter Ramutenas and Brent Hardy have provided necessary computer support.

Finally, thanks to my wife, Annette, for her support and encouragement throughout the project.

Unless otherwise noted, photographs are by the author.

1 INTRODUCTION

. . . structure is columnar, planar, or a combination of these which a designer can intentionally use to reinforce or realize ideas. In this context, columns, walls and beams can be thought of in terms of concepts of frequency, pattern, simplicity, regularity, randomness and complexity. As such, structure can be used to define space, create units, articulate circulation, suggest movement, or develop composition and modulations. In this way, it becomes inextricably linked to the very elements which create architecture, its quality and excitement.[1]

THE POTENTIAL FOR STRUCTURE TO ENRICH ARCHITECTURE

Clark and Pause's statement above begins by describing the architectural qualities of structure and then suggests how structure might enrich architecture. But is such a positive attitude to structure realistic? What was the last building *you* experienced where structure either created the architecture or contributed a sense of excitement to it? Where do we find examples of structure playing such active architectural roles as defining space and modulating surfaces? And, how else might structure contribute architecturally? These questions set the agenda of this book, informing its focus and scope and initiating an exploration of architecturally enriching structure.

Some readers may consider Clark and Pause's attitude towards structure as a fully integrated architectural element rather unrealistic. So often our day-to-day experience of structure can be described as unmemorable. In much of our built environment structure is either concealed or nondescript. Opaque façade panels or mirror-glass panes hide structure located on a building's perimeter. Inside a building, suspended ceilings conceal beams, and vertical structural elements like columns, cross-bracing and structural walls are either enveloped within partition walls or else visually indistinguishable from them. Even if structure is exposed, often its repetitive and predictable configuration in plan and elevation, as well as its unrefined member and connection detailing can rarely be described as 'creating architecture, its quality and excitement'.

Fortunately, in addition to these ubiquitous and bland structural encounters, sufficient precedents of positive structural contributions to architecture exist. They point towards bolder and more exciting possibilities and have convinced critical observers, like Clark and Pause and others, of the potential for structure to engage with architecture more actively and creatively. Peter Collins, the architectural theorist, shares similarly constructive convictions regarding structure's architectural roles. In concluding a discussion on eighteenth- and nineteenth-century rationalism, he suggests:

> However much the emphasis on structural expression may have been exaggerated in the past by a craving for ostentation, or reduced by the competing emphases on spatial effects, sculptural effects and new planning requirements, it is still potentially one of the most vigorous ideals of the modern age, and it would not be an exaggeration to say that it is the notion which offers the most fruitful prospects for the future development of modern architectural thought.[2]

Like the authors quoted above, I will also be looking beyond the physical necessity of structure towards its functional and aesthetic possibilities. Just because structure is essential for built architecture, providing it with necessary stability, strength and stiffness, it does not have to be architecturally mute – unless of course its designers make that choice. This book provides many examples of structures 'speaking' and even 'shouting' in their architectural contexts. In these cases their designers, usually both architects and structural engineers, have made structural decisions that do not detract from, but rather strengthen their architectural ideas and requirements. Structure no longer remains silent, but is a voice to be heard.

Where structure is given a voice, as illustrated in the following chapters, it contributes architectural meaning and richness, sometimes becoming the most significant of all architectural elements in a building. Endless opportunities exist for structure to enhance architecture and thereby enrich our architectural experiences. As designers we can allow structure to speak and to be heard, or to change the metaphor, we can design structure so that its viewers not only see and experience it, but due to its well-considered architectural qualities, are enticed into 'reading' it.

EXPERIENCING AND READING STRUCTURE
Architects analyse structure by experiencing and reading it. In their succinct summary, Clark and Pause suggest possible ways structure might be read, or analysed architecturally. In some architectural reviews of buildings, particularly where structure is exposed, structural readings are made. Although reviewers usually make little more than a passing

comment, the validity of this way of analysing structure remains. The following two examples illustrate architecturally focused structural readings.

Fontein offers a reading of the interior structure of her school of architecture building. She concentrates upon a single column, differentiated from others by virtue of its circular cross-section and increased height. She asserts that this column 'plays a pivotal role in the building' by marking and sheltering the intersection of two internal streets. It also connects that street junction to the school's main collective space whose activities it both supports and obstructs. Ultimately it 'establishes structure as a primary ordering device in the architecture of the School . . . and has the palpable effect of anchoring the life of the School'.[3]

LaVine tends towards less personified readings as he discerns significant architectural roles played by structure in his four house case studies.[4] He notes how a ridge beam can symbolize the social centre of a house, and how a superstructure orders space by virtue of its regularity and hierarchy. In other examples, columns 'signify human activities of special significance' or 'portray a mechanical idealism'. He reads walls as separating occupants from the outside world, and frames as ordering interior space. As he reads structure, each structural element is laden with meaning and makes an important architectural contribution.

All architectural readings incorporate a degree of subjectivity. To a certain extent, each reading is personal. It reflects a reader's background and architectural knowledge. The quality of their experience of a building is another factor which depends on the duration of a visit and the depth of reflection during and after it.

The views of two or more readers are unlikely to be identical. Each person brings their own perspective. For example, an architect and structural engineer will read a structure quite differently. Each approaches it with his or her professional interest and concerns to the forefront. Whereas an architect might focus on how structure impacts the surrounding space, an engineer will most likely perceive structure as facilitating a load-path.

So, my architectural analyses of structure, or structural readings, inevitably reflect who I am and includes my structural engineering background, my experience of teaching in a school of architecture and my intense interest in how structure can enrich architecture.

Before commencing to read building structures and explore their architectural contributions, the next section clarifies the meaning of the book's central focus, exposed structure.

STRUCTURE AND ITS DEGREE OF EXPOSURE

At this stage it is necessary to come to a common understanding of what constitutes structure, and to comment on aspects of its exposure. For the purpose of sensibly limiting the scope of the book, structure is taken as any structural element that bears load other than that arising from its self-weight or self-induced loads like those from wind or snow.

This definition excludes consideration of purely decorative elements without wanting to deny any significant architectural roles they might play. Imitative structure and authentic structural members that are not load-bearing, even though they might clearly express their materiality and display standard structural dimensions, are disregarded. Examples of the latter category include exposed frameworks whose sole purpose is to contribute to a building's composition, perhaps visually linking disparate forms together. Although this discussion omits structure whose rationale is purely aesthetic, structural elements and details with minimal structural effectiveness are included. Structural details like the attached shafts on Gothic piers fall into this category. Even though their architectural contribution may be seen as more aesthetic than structural, by increasing the cross-sectional area and depth of a pier, the details increase slightly its compression strength and overall stability.

Having established a working definition of structure, an explanation for the focus upon *exposed* structure is warranted and quite simple. Where structure is not exposed but concealed, perhaps hidden within wall cavities, screened by suspended ceilings or undifferentiated from partition walling, it possesses very limited opportunities to enrich architecture. In these situations, where the architecture must rely on other devices and elements for its qualities, any skeletal, wall-like or expressive structural qualities remain latent – structure cannot be read.

Architects take an unlimited number of approaches towards structural exposure. In its fully exposed state, the raw materiality of structure is visible, be it masonry, concrete, steel or natural timber. Even if coatings or claddings partially or fully veil structural members and their materiality, structural form can still play significant and expressive architectural roles. Steel structural members may be wrapped with corrosion and fire protection coatings and even cladding panels, but their structural forms can still enliven façades and interior spaces. Hence, in this discussion, *exposed* structure includes any visible structural forms, whether or not their materiality is concealed.

This apparent preoccupation with exposed structure does not mean it is a requirement of exemplary architecture. Exposed structure has rightly been inappropriate on many past occasions given the design ideals current at those times. Cowan gives examples of periods in architectural history, such as the Renaissance and the Baroque, where exposed structure would have detracted from the forms and embellished surfaces that designers were attempting to achieve.[5] Absence of exposed structure in contemporary buildings may also be completely defensible. For example, exterior exposed structure might compromise architectural forms exhibiting sculptural qualities and curved surfaces, and interior exposed structure could impact negatively upon an architectural goal of achieving spaces defined by pure planar surfaces.

Decisions regarding the extent to which structure should be exposed in an architectural design, if at all, are best made after revisiting the design concept and asking whether or not exposed structure will enhance its realization. Then, irrespective of the answer, design ideas will be communicated with greater clarity. Structural exposure should therefore be limited to buildings where structure integrates with and clearly strengthens the expression of architectural ideas.

BOOK OUTLINE

Chapter 2 analyses the structures of two contrasting buildings to set the scene for more focused and detailed explorations later in the book. Each building exemplifies structure contributing architecturally in the context of a specific architectural programme. Exposed structure plays significant architectural roles on the exterior of the first building, while in the second, structure creates special interior spaces. Due to the inevitably limited range of architectural contributions exemplified by the two case studies, following chapters explore and illustrate exposed structure enriching specific areas of architecture in more detail.

Beginning with Chapter 3, chapter sequencing for the remainder of the book reflects a typical progression of experiences when one visits a building. First, imagine approaching a building from a distance. When architectural massing only may be discerned, the diversity of relationship between architectural and structural form is explored. Then in Chapter 4, drawing closer to the building, one observes structural elements enlivening façades in various ways, including forming surface patterns and textures, providing visual clues of entry, connecting exterior and interior architecture, and playing diverse expressive roles.

Then having entered a building, the next three chapters attend to relationships between the structure and interior architecture. Chapter 5 examines how structure enhances and in some cases, defines building function. Structure maximizes planning flexibility, subdivides space to facilitate separate functions and articulates circulation paths. Chapter 6 focuses on interior structure as an architectural element in its own right. It addresses the question of how structure enlivens and articulates interior spaces and surfaces. Examples illustrate structure providing a wide range of surface and spatial qualities. Some interior structures read as responding to aspects such as a building's geometry or function, or alternatively, expressing external factors like soil pressures or other site-specific characteristics.

Exploration of interior structure narrows in scope in Chapter 7 by examining structural detailing. After noting the importance of detailing being driven by a design concept, examples of expressive and responsive details are provided. They comprise two categories of details, one of which gains its inspiration from within the building, and the other, from without. Some structural members are so elegantly detailed as to be considered objects of aesthetic delight, increasing one's enjoyment and interest in architecture considerably. A plethora of structural detailing languages with diverse architectural qualities strengthens designers' realization of overarching architectural design concepts.

Chapter 8 investigates the relationship between structure and light, both natural and artificial. It illustrates structure's dual roles, as both a source and modifier of light, and introduces a number of different strategies designers use to maximize the ingress of light into buildings. Chapter 9 reflects on the symbolic and representational roles structure plays. Structure references naturally occurring objects like trees and processes such as erosion, as well as human artifacts, and notions and experiences as diverse as oppression and humour. The final chapter concludes with a brief distillation of the main themes that emerge throughout the book, namely the transformative power of structure, the diversity with which it enriches architecture, and implications for the architectural and structural engineering professions.

REFERENCES AND NOTES

1   Clark, R. H. and Pause, M. (1985). *Precedents in Architecture*. Van Nostrand Reinhold, p. 3.

2   Collins, P. (1998). *Changing Ideals in Modern Architecture 1750–1950*, 2nd edn. McGill–Queens University Press, p. 217.

3   Fontein, L. (2000). Reading structure through the frame. *Perspecta 31*, MIT Press, pp. 50–9.

4   LaVine, L. (2001). *Mechanics and Meaning in Architecture*. University of Minnesota Press.

5   Cowan, H. (1980). A note on structural honesty. *Architecture Australia*, Feb./March, pp. 28–32.

2 TWO BUILDING STUDIES

This chapter analyses the structures of two very different buildings. Between them they exemplify structure enriching most aspects and areas of architecture. It prepares the way for a more detailed investigation and categorization of the architectural potential of structure in subsequent chapters.

The following two building studies illustrate the considered use of exposed structure in very different architectural contexts. First, the BRIT School, London, is considered. While it displays an exuberant exterior structure, its structure as experienced from the interior adopts a more utilitarian stance. Roles reverse in the second building, the Baumschulenweg Crematorium, with its impressive exposed interior structure. Within a formal minimalist exterior envelope, large 'randomly placed' interior columns transform the main interior space, imbuing it with feeling and meaning.

BRITISH RECORD INDUSTRY TRUST (BRIT) SCHOOL

Located in Croydon, London, the BRIT School educates students in the performing arts and related skills. As the curriculum was still under development during the building design process, interior space had to be flexible enough to accommodate changing needs, including future expansion, yet incorporate an acoustically separated theatre and sound studios.

The architectural form embodies these programmatic requirements in a central three-storey core surrounded by a two-storey podium. Two contrasting structural systems, the load-bearing core and an exoskeletal framework, support the architectural form (Fig. 2.1). They are both equally responsive to the building programme. Heavy and relatively massive, the reinforced concrete masonry core satisfies acoustic requirements. From its corners, four primary roof trusses cantilever toward external piers located beyond the building envelope, and secondary trusses bear on its side walls to leave the first floor completely free of interior columns.

▲ **2.1**   BRIT School, Croydon, London, England, Cassidy Taggart Partnership, 1991. Exoskeleton with the core behind the two-storey podium. Ventilation ducts protrude from the core wall.

▲ **2.2**   Free-standing masonry piers in front of the building.

The two free-standing concrete masonry piers at the front and back of the building claim space likely to be incorporated into the building at a future date (Fig. 2.2). Spaced 20 m apart, too wide to signify entry explicitly, their placement approximates the width of the double-height entry atrium behind them. Eight smaller but similarly tapered piers, some placed well away from the existing building envelope where it steps back in plan towards the core, provide for anticipated outwards expansion (Fig. 2.3). They support steel frames, some of whose trussed

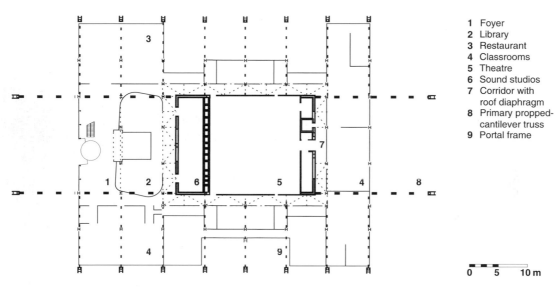

1 Foyer
2 Library
3 Restaurant
4 Classrooms
5 Theatre
6 Sound studios
7 Corridor with
 roof diaphragm
8 Primary propped-
 cantilever truss
9 Portal frame

▲ **2.3** Simplified ground floor plan.

▲ **2.4** Partial portal frames span between the piers and the primary trusses or core walls.

rafters connect directly to the core, and others to the primary can-tilever trusses (Fig. 2.4). Slender longitudinal tubes interconnect the partial portal frames at their knee-joints, and together with a mesh of small-diameter tension rods, brace the framework members back to the core.

▲ **2.5** Exterior column recessed within an external wall.

Exposed structure plays numerous architectural roles on the exterior. Along the building, the piers and the steel columns they support are separated clearly from the building envelope. They modulate and enliven exterior walls with their visual mass and diverse materiality. The piers and portal frames define and limit the eventual extent of the expanded building footprint by defining the edges of potential infill spaces. The combination of masonry construction and pier tapering that expresses structural resistance to the outward thrusts from the portal columns suggests a buttressing action. This intensifies a sense of perimeter structure confining, protecting and supporting the two-storey podium. Steel trusses above roof level conceptually as well as structurally tie these external structural elements back to the core, which itself anchors the building visually and physically against lateral loads.

Exterior ground floor columns that support the first floor composite steel–concrete slab are recessed within light timber-clad walls (Fig. 2.5). These exposed columns and their bolted beam connections indicate the post-and-beam nature of the interior structure and provide advance notice of how well interior columns are generally integrated with partition walls. An absence of first floor columns on exterior wall lines emphasizes that the roof is supported by the exterior structure that spans the space between the perimeter and the core, providing column-free interior planning flexibility.

At the ground floor, interior columns placed on a repetitive rectangular grid allow for a satisfactory level of functionality. Almost all columns are positioned within interior walls. Spatial planning is well integrated with structural layout. Unfortunately, in two locations adjacent to walls surrounding the library, columns sit awkwardly in the circulation space. They disrupt both the expectation and the physical experience of walking around the gently curved flanking walls. Otherwise, structure, together with partition walls, defines interior spaces and circulation routes, the most prominent of which hug the core.

The architects have chosen to expose all interior columns, beams, the suspended floor soffit, and mechanical and electrical services. While this strategy typifies a tight budget it allows for ease of future adaptation. Design decisions have led to a celebratory exterior structure at the expense of more utilitarian structural detailing inside.

While structural detailing quality varies enormously from inside to out, innovative exterior steel detailing deserves special mention. Detailing of the tapered steel columns that rise from clearly articulated pin joints is most distinctive and original (Fig. 2.6). A steel hollow-section that is welded to a thin vertical and stiffened plate forms the column

▲ 2.6   Innovatively detailed portal frame columns, with the core and an 'anvil' support for the trusses in the background.

cross-section. Increasing the depth of the column with height expresses how the structural bending moment profile reaches its peak at the knee-joint. Outer areas of the thin steel plate furthest away from the hollow-section are suited to resisting gravity-load bending moment tension stresses. The radial and perpendicular orientated triangular stiffening plates enable the gravity-load tensile stresses to be carried around the corner of the knee-joint without the thin plate buckling radially, and increase the plate's compression capability under wind uplift conditions. As well as celebrating steel materiality and expressing structural actions, the column detailing exemplifies creativity and innovation. Contrast the quality of this detailing with a more typical solution comprising standard off-the-shelf universal column and beam sections!

After the columns 'bend' from a vertical to a horizontal orientation at their rigid knee-joints, their graceful transformation from steel plate and hollow-section form into trussed-rafters exemplify another innovative detail. The vocabulary of steel plates and hollow-sections expands with the addition of further unconventional details in the primary propped cantilevered trusses. At the point where they are propped by the external piers, steel truss members thicken and forfeit their sense of materiality. They could be either steel or precast concrete (Fig. 2.7). At the other end of the truss another detailing language appears – bolted side-plates with circular penetrations (Fig. 2.8). Such a diversity of structural languages can sometimes have a detrimental effect on achieving a visually unified structure, but in this building which celebrates creativity, the white painted steelwork provides sufficient visual continuity.

▲ **2.7**   Detail of a primary truss to pier connection.

▲ **2.8**   Primary truss near its connection to the core.

Adjacent to the masonry core walls, primary truss top-chord cross-sections change from steel hollow-sections to three tension rods. Articulating their state of tension clearly, they curve over a steel anvil-like support on the top of the core and continue horizontally through an intermediate support to meet an identical truss chord from the other end of the building (see Fig. 2.6). Although the horizontal rods are more highly visible when drawn on plan than seen on site due to their lightness of colour, their continuity along the length of the core walls expresses how the primary trusses counteract to support each other. They cantilever in a reasonably balanced fashion from each end of the core. Instead of burying the horizontal rods within the core walls, the architects articulate equal and opposite tension forces, and thereby intensify the visual richness of the exposed structure.

While generally less refined constructionally than their exterior counterparts, several interior structural members have benefited from special detailing treatment. Perhaps acknowledging the importance of first impressions, fine steel tapered-plate mullions and beams support the atrium wall glazing and the main entry canopy. This fineness of detailing also strengthens the visual link between exterior and interior structure (Fig. 2.9).

Natural light reaches deep inside the building through glazed roof areas over the corridors around the core perimeter. A similar pattern of narrower slots through the first floor slab enables light to penetrate to ground floor level. Daylight first passes through the exterior roof structure, and then through the diagonal in-plane roof and floor diaphragm bracing. But neither structural system modifies the light quality or quantity significantly. Structural openness and fineness, and its wide spacing minimizes any such influence (Fig. 2.10). Rather than the structure disrupting

▲ **2.9** Refined structural detailing in the atrium and to the main entrance canopy.

light, light highlights the structure. One is therefore more conscious than ever of these diagonal members in the floor plane and the roof. As they brace all outlying roof and floor areas back to the core to ensure the lateral stability of the podium, their diagonal geometry contrasts with the orthogonal ordering of the primary structure.

Finally, this analysis of the BRIT School explores the representational and symbolic roles of structure. The contrast between a heavy and strong core and the podium's lightness and relative fragility might read as expressing the relative importance of theatrical performance in the school's life. The physical separation and visual differentiation of structure from the cladding might also be seen as an invitation and opportunity for future expansion. However, a more compelling example of meaning embodied in this structure resides in the detailing of the exterior structure, particularly the steel columns. Whereas 'visually emphasized or High-Tech structure' has been interpreted as expressing ideals of technical progress, in this case innovative structural detailing expresses the school's role of developing and fostering creativity.[1] This reading of the structure is not new. In the early years of the school, images of exterior columns featured on its letterhead.

BAUMSCHULENWEG CREMATORIUM

After proceeding through the gatehouse of the Berlin suburban cemetery and following a short walk along a tree-lined forecourt, visitors confront the symmetrical low-rise form of the crematorium. An

▲ **2.10** Roof and first floor diaphragm bracing.

▲ **2.11**   Crematorium, Baumschulenweg, Berlin, Germany, Axel Schultes Architects, 1999. Front elevation.

absence of exterior doors and conventional fenestration or other visual clues creates uncertainty in interpreting the building's scale (Fig. 2.11). Although the façade composition is read as single-storey, up to three storeys are accommodated above the main ground-floor level. Planar concrete elements in the form of perimeter walls, a raised ground floor and a roof slab define the rectilinear form.

Even from a distance, visitors become aware of the roof slab discontinuity. Above the two side-entry portals a roof slot reveals a glimpse of sky that one commentator refers to as 'a harbinger of the end of grief.'[2] These longitudinal slots continue through to the other end of the building. They slice the building into three independent structures even though common materiality and consistency of architectural language unite them visually. The outer two zones, to use Louis Khan's terminology, 'serve' the major central area that accommodates three chapels and a condolence hall (Fig. 2.12).

Walls dominate the exterior elevations, functioning as both structure and cladding. Side walls initially read as approximately 2 m thick, but in fact they are hollow – doors from the entry portals lead to rooms within the 'walls'. Elsewhere, relatively thin edges of exposed walls and slabs express the dominant structural language of wall that is repeated within the interior box-like modules that enclose one large and two smaller chapels. Ceiling slabs over these three spaces are also slotted, allowing light to enter through louvred glazing. Gentle curved ends to the ceiling slabs relieve an otherwise rigid adherence to orthogonality.

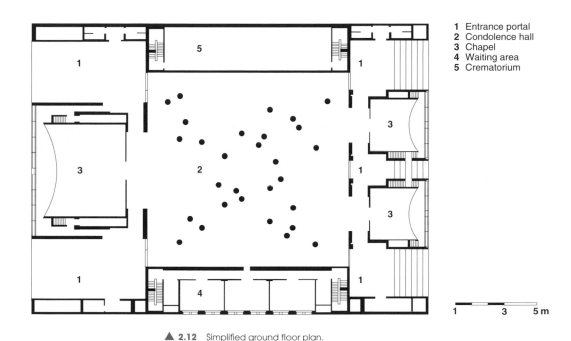

1 Entrance portal
2 Condolence hall
3 Chapel
4 Waiting area
5 Crematorium

1   3   5 m

▲ **2.12** Simplified ground floor plan.

▲ **2.13** Condolence hall columns.

A study of the main floor plan indicates tripartite longitudinal subdivision – front and back porticoes and chapel spaces lie at each end of the centrally located condolence hall. Structural walls that are generously penetrated with openings at ground floor level separate and screen the chapels from the hall. Within each longitudinal zone, structural walls subdivide space transversely. In the middle zone, walls delineate the condolence hall from the side waiting rooms and the crematorium. In the front and back zones, walls play similar roles by separating circulation and services spaces from the chapels. Structural walls therefore dominate the plan, delineating the various functions. Only within the condolence hall have the architects introduced another structural language.

Columns comprise the primary architectural elements of this large interior volume (Fig. 2.13). Their presence, together with an unusual lighting strategy, results in a space with a special ambiance that is well suited to its function. The 'random' placement of columns recalls the spatial qualities of a native forest rather than an orderly plantation. Scattered large-diameter columns disrupt obvious linear circulation routes between destinations beyond the hall. One must meander. Tending to cluster in plan along diagonal bands, columns subdivide the main floor area into four relatively large spaces, and many others that are smaller and ideal for groups of two to three people. Differently sized and shaped open areas become gathering places.

One of the largest 'places' is located in front of the main chapel. Dwarfed by massive, 11m high columns, mourners meet to console one another. Columns either facilitate this interaction by virtue of their enclosing presence or provide opportunities for anonymity. They remind visitors of their human frailty, yet might even be a source of reassurance given their physical and symbolic qualities of strength and protection. Their scale instils a sense of awe rather than of intimidation.

The scale of the condolence hall and its columns, as well as its low light levels, recalls hyperstyle construction, both in its original Egyptian setting and in more accessible locations, such as in the basement of L'Institute du Monde Arabe, Paris. But, whereas hypostyle column layout conforms to a rigidly ordered square grid, the crematorium column placement can be described as unpredictable.

Here, the grid has disappeared. According to Balmond, with columns free of the grid, space is no longer 'dull and uninspired'. He describes how, during the design process, two rows of columns were 'freed-up' in a gallery hall at the Rotterdam Kunsthal by 'sliding' one row past the other in an 'out-of-phase shift': 'Suddenly the room was liberated. Diagonals opened up the floor plan and the room became one space, not two ring-fenced zones . . .'[3] By comparison with columns at the Kunsthal, those at the crematorium enjoy far more freedom even though they remain straight and are vertical.

A masterly introduction of natural light intensifies this powerful and surprising experience of interior structure. At each roof slab-to-column junction, an area of critical structural connectivity, an annulus interrupted only by a narrow concrete beam allows natural light to wash down the column surfaces (Fig. 2.14). Daylight illumines longitudinal side walls similarly. Slots adjacent to walls disconnect the roof slab from its expected source of support. Just where shear forces are normally greatest, the slab stops short, cantilevering from the nearest columns. Light enters through the slots and illuminates and reflects off the structure (Fig. 2.15). The conventional grey cast-in-place concrete of walls, columns and roof slab combines with intentionally low light levels to heighten a sense of solemnity and calmness.

Unlike the BRIT School with its diversity of structural materials, its structural hierarchy and celebratory detailing, the crematorium's structural drama and interest results primarily from structural simplicity, generosity of scale and its configuration. Structural detailing can be

▲ **2.14** Annuli of light as column 'capitals'.

▲ **2.15** Light-slot between the side wall and the roof slab.

described as plain. Columns are of identical diameter with an off-the-form surface finish. As plain cylinders, lacking a pedestal or a capital other than the annulus of light, they emerge starkly from the stone floor surfacing at their bases to fuse monolithically with the beam stubs and the flat planar roof slab soffit above. Surface textures relieve wall surfaces. Formwork tie holes and regularly spaced positive joints, as opposed to more conventional negative formwork joints, modulate large wall areas. Regular vertical niches spaced along the condolence hall longitudinal walls play a similar role (Fig. 2.16).

Minimalist structural detailing denies any expression of structural actions. Uniform column size belies the different loads supported by each. Columns that are well separated in plan from other columns bear heavy compressive loads while due to slab structural continuity, some closely spaced columns experience minimal compression. Although these lightly laden columns could have been removed during the design process by simply modifying the slab reinforcing layout, an apparent increase in structural efficiency by decreasing column numbers would have diminished architectural aspirations. Similarly, a reluctance to taper the slab depth in those areas where it cantilevers, indicates the preciousness of a simple and solemn orthogonal architectural language.

The interior structure of the condolence hall exemplifies the potential for structure to enrich interior architecture both aesthetically and functionally. 'Random' column layout, structural scale commensurate with volume, and interaction of structure and light enliven a large volume,

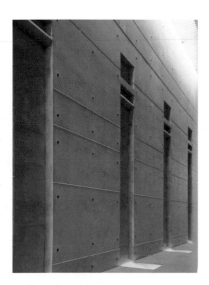

▲ **2.16** Texture and niches of the condolence hall side-walls.

stimulating a variety of reactions and emotions, and actively facilitating its intended use.

Summary

These studies of the BRIT School and the Baumschulenweg Crematorium begin to illustrate the potential of structure to enrich architecture. While the exterior structure of the school makes significant aesthetic contributions, interior structure is notable only at the crematorium. Although both structures convey meaning, the contrast in how one reads and experiences them is striking. As the relationship between architectural form and structural form is investigated in the next chapter, the diversity of experience that structure offers continues to surprise.

REFERENCES AND NOTES

1   Macdonald, A. J. (1997). *Structural Design for Architecture*. Architectural Press, p. 32.
2   Russell, J. S. (2000). Evoking the infinite. *Architectural Record*, 05:00, 224–31.
3   Balmond, C. (2002). *informal*. Prestel, p. 79.

3

Relationships between architectural and structural form

INTRODUCTION

This chapter is the first of seven that imagine visiting a building and progressively exploring in greater detail the roles structure plays in various areas and aspects of its architecture. As such it observes and reflects on architectural issues arising essentially *outside* the building. From a location some distance away, the form or massing of the building, rather than any exterior detail, dominates visually and invites an exploration of the relationships between architectural and structural form. But before considering the diversity of relationships between these forms that designers can exploit for the sake of architectural enrichment, the meaning of several terms require clarification.

Architectural form is often used but less frequently defined. Ching breaks from the tradition of using the term loosely. Yet, although he defines it explicitly, his definition still remains imprecise. He suggests that architectural form is an inclusive term that refers primarily to a building's external outline or shape, and to a lesser degree references its internal organization and unifying principles. He also notes that *shape* encompasses various visual and relational properties; namely size, colour and texture, position, orientation and visual inertia.[1] Form, in his view, is therefore generally and primarily understood as the shape or three-dimensional massing, but also encompasses additional architectural aspects including structural configuration and form, in so far as they may organize and unify an architectural design.

For the purpose of this discussion, architectural form is essentially understood as and limited to enveloping form, or shape. This deliberate simplification and clarification conceptually excludes from architectural form any consideration of interior and exterior structural organization. It acknowledges the fact that three-dimensional massing may be completely unrelated to structural form. By decoupling structure from the rather nebulous but conventional usage of architectural form, opportunities are provided to examine structure's relationships to specific aspects of architecture included previously within more general definitions of architectural form. These aspects include issues such as texture, order and spatial organization. This limited definition of architectural form, exclusive of structural considerations, also reflects observations of both the reality of architectural design approaches and the built architecture discussed in this chapter. In the design process, within architectural practice and buildings themselves, separation between architectural and structural forms is commonplace. The two distinctive structural forms in the Baumschulenweg Crematorium have already been observed. Walls that relate closely to the architectural form, and columns that do not, both coexist within the building envelope and contribute richly to its exterior and interior architecture respectively.

Structural form also requires elaboration. In the context of architectural writing its traditional usage usually conveys the structural essence of a building. For example, the structural form of a post-and-beam structure might be described as skeletal, even though the posts and beams might support planar floor structure and are stabilized by shear walls. In this case the observer perceives the structural framework as the dominant structural system in the building. Perhaps the framework is a more visually pronounced element than the shear walls. Visibility of the framework's elements, its beams and columns, is in all likelihood enhanced by an absence of interior partitions, while the shear walls recede into the background.

This book generally understands structural form as a building's primary or most visually dominant structural system. While most buildings have several primary structural systems, some have only one. Library Square, Vancouver is one such example (Fig. 3.1). Moment-resisting frames running at regular intervals across the plan resist gravity and longitudinal lateral loads, and two perimeter frames resist transverse lateral loads.

Most buildings contain two or three structural systems – either a gravity-load resisting system and one or two systems that resist lateral loads in both orthogonal directions, or a combined gravity and uni-directional lateral load system complimented by another system for lateral loads in the orthogonal direction. The Mont-Cenis Academy, Herne, exemplifies the first configuration (see Figs 3.26 and 3.27). Continuous roof trusses on pole columns resist gravity loads while steel rod cross-bracing in the roof plane and along each of the four exterior walls withstands lateral loads. Exchange House, London, typifies the second situation, comprising two different lateral load resisting systems. Arches, stiffened by diagonal ties,

▲ **3.1** Library Square, Vancouver, Canada, Moshe Safdie and Associates Inc., 1995. A typical longitudinal frame and the end of a perimeter transverse frame.

resist gravity and longitudinal loads, and exposed cross-bracing resists transverse loads (see Figs 3.40 and 3.41).

In buildings with more than one structural system and where it is unclear which system is primary from a visual perspective, the concept of *structural form* is too simplistic. The term *structural systems* is more appropriate in these cases.

Suckle's study of ten leading architects suggests that architects determine building form after considering a wide range of factors that usually, in the first instance, do not include structure.[2] Design issues such as integrating the programme or brief within the allowable site coverage and budget all within an overriding architectural concept tend to be dealt with first. She finds that while the intensity and importance of an initial design concept varies greatly from designer to designer, structural considerations are never paramount during the initial design stage to determine building massing. Many architects probably identify with Erickson when he states:

> *Structure is the strongest and most powerful element of form, so much so that if it is not the last consideration in the long series of decisions determining form, it distorts or modifies all other determinants of a building. One finds in fact, that the structure has dictated all the other aspects of the design. The inhabitants should not behave as the columns dictate – the contrary should surely be the case . . . As with all my buildings the structure was not even considered until the main premises of the design – the shape of the spaces and the form of the building had been determined. Thus, the structure did not preclude but followed the design intent.[3]*

It is worth noting that although Erickson postpones structural decisions in the early design stages, his architecture is notable for its rational and clearly expressed structure. His buildings lack any evidence of conceptual structural design decisions being left too late in the design process, resulting in structure poorly integrated with building function and aesthetics. One just needs to recall his Vancouver Law Courts building and the Museum of Anthropology, University of British Columbia, Vancouver, to appreciate the clarity with which structure 'speaks' in his architecture.

Such an attitude towards structure as 'form-follower' rather than 'form-giver' contrasts starkly with opposing views that have been articulated in various periods of architectural history. For example, Viollet-le-Duc expressed the views of eighteenth-century Structural Rationalists: 'Impose on me a structural system, and I will naturally find you the forms which should result from it. But if you change the structure, I shall be obliged to change the forms.'[4] He spoke with Gothic architecture in mind, where masonry load-bearing walls and buttresses comprise the building envelope. By virtue of its large plan area and its exterior and interior spatial impact, structure so dominates Gothic construction that a close relationship exists between structural and architectural form. However, since the eighteenth century and the advent of high-strength tension-capable materials like iron and then steel, the previously limited structural vocabulary of walls, vaults and buttresses has been extended greatly and often been relieved of the task of enveloping buildings. Newer systems like moment frames and cantilever columns are common, and these are used in conjunction with modern non-structural enveloping systems such as precast concrete and light-weight panels. Building enclosure is now frequently separated from the structure to the extent that the structural form may be quite unexpected given the architectural form.

Viollet-le-Duc's beliefs in structure as 'form-giver' were reaffirmed just as forcefully in the 1950s by Pier Luigi Nervi:

> Moreover, I am deeply convinced – and this conviction is strengthened by a critical appraisal of the most significant architectural works of the past as well as of the present – that the outward appearance of a good building cannot, and must not, be anything but the visible expression of an efficient structural or constructional reality. In other words, form must be the necessary result, and not the initial basis of structure.[5]

Nervi's view, persuasive only in the context of high-rise and long-span construction, is supported by Glasser: 'as in the case of arenas, auditoriums, and stadiums – it is equally clear that a conceptual design without a rigorous and well-integrated structural framework would be specious.'[6]

The following sections of this chapter illustrate the diversity of rela-tionships between architectural and structural forms. Works of archi-tecture where architectural and structural forms synthesize are first examined. Then, after considering the most commonly encountered situation where the relationships between the forms can be considered consonant, the chapter finally moves to examples of buildings where, for various reasons, architectural and structural forms contrast.

The order in which the three relationships are discussed is not intended to imply a preference towards any one of them in particular. No rela-tionship between architectural and structural form, be it synthesis, con-sonant or contrast, is inherently better than another. What *is* of utmost importance, however, is the degree to which structure, whatever its relationship to architectural form, contributes to a successful realiza-tion of architectural design aspirations.

SYNTHESIS OF ARCHITECTURAL AND STRUCTURAL FORM

This section considers seven structural systems that typically exemplify a synthesis between architectural and structural form. In these cases structure defines architectural form and often functions, at least partially, as the building envelope. The order in which the structural systems are discussed begins with shell structures that of all structural systems most closely integrate the two forms. The remaining systems then generally follow a progression from curved to more linear and planar forms.

Shell structures

Shell structures achieve the most pure synthesis of architectural and structural forms. Also known as 'surface structures', shells resist and transfer loads within their minimal thicknesses. They rely upon their three-dimensional curved geometry and correct orientation and place-ment of supports for their adequate structural performance. When con-structed from reinforced concrete, many shells, such as those designed by Isler, a leading European concrete shell designer, reveal smooth curved surfaces inside and out, much like those of a hen's egg.[7] Isler's shells unify architectural and structural form as they spring from their foundations and continuously curve over to envelop interior space (Fig. 3.2).

At the Palazzetto dello Sport, Rome, the shell surface does not meet the foundations directly but ends at the eaves level where inclined struts resist the outward thrusts (Fig. 3.3). This shell also defines the roof form, functioning simultaneously as structure and enclosure. Its interior surfaces are ribbed (Fig. 3.4). Interlacing ribs that evidence its precast concrete formwork segments both increase shell stability and achieve a much admired structural texture.

▲ **3.2**   Interior of a concrete shell structure. (Courtesy J. Chilton)

▲ **3.3**   Palazzetto dello Sport, Rome, Italy, Pier Luigi Nervi with A Vitellozzi, 1957. Inclined struts support the shell roof.

▲ **3.4**   Interior ribbed surface of the shell.

▲ **3.5**   Eden Project, Cornwall, England, Nicholas Grimshaw & Partners, 2001. A cluster of interlinked biomes.

Shell structures can also be constructed from linear steel or timber members, as in the cases of geodesic or other braced domes. Although in these cases the many short structural members shape a faceted structural surface which must then be clad, structure nonetheless defines architectural form. The huge greenhouses of the Eden Project, Cornwall, are such examples (Fig. 3.5). Hexagons, a geometrical pattern found in many naturally occurring structures, are the building blocks of these shells, or biomes as they are called. Due to the long spans of up to 124 m, the outer primary hexagonal steel structure is supplemented by a secondary inner layer of tension rods (Fig. 3.6). By increasing structural depths of the biomes like this, the diameters of the main hexagon tubes could be more than halved to less than 200 mm, considerably

▲ **3.6**   Biome interior structure consisting of outer primary hexagons and an inner layer of braced rods.

▲ **3.7**   Stellingen Ice Skating Rink and Velodrome, Hamburg, Germany, Silcher, Werner + Partners, 1996. Overall form.

improving their overall transparency. The biomes demonstrate the degree of synthesis of forms possible with shell structures. Although in this project structure acts as building skin in a very minor way, it defines an organic architectural form whilst achieving rational, economic and transparent construction.

Fabric structures

Fabric or membrane structures represent another type of surface structure. These structures, where tensioned fabric initially resists self-weight and other loads, also rely upon their three-dimensional curvatures for structural adequacy. Fabric form, thickness and strength must match the expected loads, and all surfaces must be stretched taut to prevent the fabric flapping during high winds. Like shell structures, there is no distinction between the architectural and the structural forms. Fabric structures, however, require additional and separate compression members to create high-points over which the fabric can be stretched. Arches, with their curved forms, are well suited and aesthetically the most sympathetic to the curving fabric geometry, but masts, flying struts and cables which are more common, introduce dissimilar geometric forms and materiality. Their linearity, density and solidity contrast with the flowing double-curved, light-weight and translucent fabric surfaces, and can sometimes visually disturb the fabric's overall softness of form.

At the Stellingen Ice Skating Rink and Velodrome, Hamburg, four masts that project through the fabric and connect to it by tension cables provide the primary means of compression support (Fig. 3.7). Eight flying struts provide additional high points. From interior cables tensioned between the four outermost masts they thrust upward into the fabric

▲ **3.8** Contrasting architectural qualities of fabric surface and interior structural elements.

to increase its curvature and improve its structural performance. The building interior illustrates clearly the different architectural qualities of the fabric and its linear supporting structure – masts, flying struts and interior steel cables (Fig. 3.8).

Catenaries

Catenary structures, like fabric structures, transfer loads to their supports through tension. The simplest example of a catenary is a draped cable spanning between two high points. Catenaries that support roofs are usually designed so that the roof self-weight exceeds the wind suction or uplift pressures that would otherwise cause excessive vertical movement. Reinforced concrete is sometimes chosen as a catenary material for this reason. The concrete encases the tension steel protectively and provides the exterior and interior surfaces. Lighter catenary systems are possible provided that wind uplift is overcome with ballast or a separate tie-down system. Catenary tension members are usually distinct from the cladding and exposed within or outside the building envelope. The Portuguese Pavilion canopy, Lisbon, and Hall 26 of the Trade Fair, Hanover, illustrate these two approaches.

At the southern end of the Portuguese Pavilion, built for Expo '98, a ceremonial plaza 65 m long by 58 m wide is sheltered by a 200 mm thick reinforced concrete catenary slab. It has been variously described as a 'veil' or 'tent' on account of its remarkable slimness and draped form (Fig. 3.9). Two porticoes, one at each end, act as massive end-blocks to resist the catenary tension. Within each portico, nine parallel walls or

▲ **3.9**   Portuguese Pavilion, Lisbon, Portugal, Alvaro Siza, 1998. The canopy drapes between two porticoes.

▲ **3.10**   Dulles International Airport, Washington, DC, USA, Saarinen (Eero) and Associates, 1962. Inclined piers support the catenary slab.

buttresses resist the large inwards pull from the hanging slab. Its simplicity of detailing carries through to the design of the porticoes which are not at all expressive of their important structural roles. Their simple orthogonality would have been compromised if the common procedure of tapering buttress walls in acknowledgement of the reduction of their bending moments with height had been undertaken. The piers of the Dulles International Airport Terminal, Washington, DC, illustrate the usual approach. Their tapering as well as their inclination express the strain of supporting a heavy reinforced concrete roof (Fig. 3.10).

The Portuguese Pavilion plaza shelter therefore consists of two forms, the catenary and the porticoes. Both, simple and plain, exemplify synthesis of architectural and structural form. (Chapter 6 examines the novel detail of exposed catenary tendons at a portico-to-slab junction.)

Undulating waves formed by alternating masts and catenary roofs at Hall 26, Hanover, also demonstrate totally integrated architectural and structural forms (Fig. 3.11). In stark contrast to the solid concrete porticoes of the Portuguese Pavilion, the triangulated and trestle-like masts possess architectural qualities of lightness and transparency. Within the main interior spaces the structural steel catenary members that read as 'tension bands' support the roof and timber ceiling, or in selected areas, glazed roof panels (Fig. 3.12).

Ribbed structures

Ribbed structures can also become almost synonymous with enclosure where they generate and define architectural form, although their skeletal character often necessitates a separate enveloping system. Ribs usually cantilever from their foundations or are propped near their

▲ **3.11**   Hall 26, Trade Fair, Hanover, Germany, Herzog + Partner, 1996. Three catenaries span between masts.

▲ **3.12**   Exposed steel catenary members connect to an interior mast.

bases. If ribs are inclined from the vertical or curved in elevation they may be propped by other ribs to achieve equilibrium, as in the case of a ribbed dome. Ribbed structures generally enclose single volumes rather than multi-storey construction. By restricting the height of these structures effectively to a single storey, albeit very high, designers avoid potentially compromising a pure architectural language of ribs with additional interior load-bearing structure.

Ribs visually dominate each of the four structurally independent Licorne football stadium perimeter walls at Amiens (Fig. 3.13). Elegantly curved and tapered, the ribs shelter the spectators and accentuate a sense of enclosure. The combination of widely spaced ribs and glazing provides an unusually high degree of transparency and openness – daylight is maximized, spectators are more acutely aware than usual that the game is being played outside, and they can enjoy the surrounding townscape.

A prop near to the base of each rib provides its base-fixity and stability in the transverse direction. Unusually configured moment-resisting frames within the ribbed surface resist longitudinal loads. In these frames the ribs function as columns, and the horizontal tubes or girts, rigidly connected at 1 m spacing up the ribs, as beams (Fig. 3.14). The integration of girts with ribs to form these multi-bay frames avoids the need for a more common and economical form of resistance, such as diagonal bracing whose geometry would clash with an otherwise regular orthogonal pattern of ribs and girts.

A similar combination of primary structural ribs and secondary horizontal tubes defines the architectural form of the Reichstag Cupola, Berlin (Fig. 3.15). In this case, ribs lean against each other via a crowning compression ring. An internal double-helical ramp structure supported off

▲ **3.13** Licorne Soccer Stadium, Amiens, France, Chaix & Morel et Associés, 1999. Curved ribbed walls enclose the pitch and spectators.

▲ **3.14** Wall ribs, props and longitudinal girts.

▲ **3.15** The Reichstag Cupola, Berlin, Germany, Foster and Partners, 1999. Radial ribs and circumferential tubes.

▲ **3.16** Ludwig Erhard House, Berlin, Germany, Nicholas Grimshaw & Partners, 1998. Arched end of building as seen from the rear.

the ribs provides them with additional horizontal stiffness through its in-plan ring-beam action. A circumferential moment-resisting frame similar to that of the Licorne Stadium lies within the dome surface to resist lateral loads.

Arches

Arches also offer a potential synthesis of architectural and structural form. At Ludwig Erhard House, Berlin (Fig. 3.16) repeated arches

▲ **3.17**   The Great Glasshouse, Carmarthenshire, Wales, Foster and Partners, 1998. Arched roof.

structure a vault-like building form. Varying arch spans respond to an irregularly shaped site. Suspended floors either hang from tension hangers under the arches, or as on the street frontage, are propped off them. This is an example of reasonably conventional arch usage where arches are regularly spaced and aligned vertically. But at the Great Glasshouse, Carmarthenshire, arches form a toroidal dome (Fig. 3.17). The dome's two constant orthogonal radii of curvature require that the arches distant from the building's centreline lean over in response to the three-dimensional surface curvature. Clarity of the arched structural form is undiminished by the small diameter tubes that run longitudinally to tie the arches back at regular intervals to a perimeter ring beam. Apart from supporting the roof glazing they also prevent the arches from buckling laterally and deflecting from their inclined planes.

Framed structures

Synthesis of architectural and structural form extends beyond curved forms. Consider the intimate relationship between orthogonal skeletal structural frameworks and rectilinear forms. In his discussion of the formative 1891 Sears Roebuck Store in Chicago, Condit asserts: 'for the first time the steel and wrought-iron skeleton became fully and unambiguously the means of architectonic expression . . . The long west elevation is developed directly out of the structural system behind it, much as the isolated buttresses of the Gothic Cathedral serve as primary visual elements in its indissoluble unity of structure and form.'[8]

▲ **3.18**   La Grande Arche, Paris, France, Johan Otto van Spreckelsen, 1989. Frames within a frame.

▲ **3.19**   An interior vierendeel truss to the right.

Most orthogonal beam-column frameworks integrate well within prismatic architectural forms. The ubiquitous medium- to high-rise office building is a typical example, but even though exemplifying integrated architectural and structural forms the ensuing architecture may not be meritorious. The following three rather unusual but well-regarded buildings illustrate the realization of and the potential for synthesizing frames and architectural form.

La Grande Arche, Paris, itself a huge open frame when viewed in frontal elevation, comprises a hierarchy of frames (Fig. 3.18). Along each leg of the frame four equally spaced five-storey internal mega-frames rise to support the roof. Each mega-frame storey is subdivided into seven intermediate floor levels. The long-span roof and the plinth structure that spans over numerous subterranean tunnels are also framed – in the form of three-storey deep vierendeel trusses. Similar secondary roof frames at right-angles to the primary trusses form a grillage in plan from which to cantilever the chamfered roof and plinth edges. Vierendeel truss elements are exposed within the roof exhibition areas. Although their chamfered top-chord sections and their chord-to-web haunches depart from the orthogonality of most of the structure they do resonate with the overall chamfered building form (Fig. 3.19).

Uncompromising orthogonal rigour characterizes the cubic form and perimeter frames of the San Cataldo Cemetery columbarium, or chamber for remains at Modena (Fig. 3.20). From both architectural and structural engineering perspectives, the exterior surfaces that are penetrated by unglazed openings can also be considered as highly pierced walls, given their plastered smoothness and an absence of any articulation of individual beam or column members. The frame thickness, exaggerated by the depth of the integral ossuary compartments, reinforces ideas of hollowness and

▲ **3.20**   San Cataldo Cemetery columbarium, Modena, Italy, Aldo Rossi, 1984. Rigorous orthogonality.

▲ **3.21**   Princess of Wales Conservatory, London, England, Gordon Wilson, 1986. Pitched portal frame variations.

emptiness that are reminiscent of empty eye sockets in a skull. This reading corresponds with an understanding of the work as an 'unfinished, deserted house, a built metaphor of death'.[9] The building interior is also essentially hollow, except for stairs and galleries on a skeletal steel framework with contrasting scaffolding-like qualities.

Pitched portal frames consisting of two columns connected rigidly to sloping rafters structure innumerable light-industrial and other utilitarian buildings. This structural form that rarely graces the pages of architectural publications, integrates with architectural form in the Princess of Wales Conservatory, London. In realizing a 'glazed hill' design concept, the architect manipulates basic multi-bay portals (Fig. 3.21). However, unlike most portal frames, the side rafters connect directly to the perimeter foundations, successfully reducing the building's visual impact on its surroundings. The form-generating portals that span transversely are geometrically simple but subtle transformations that introduce asymmetry and volumetric complexity distance the conservatory from its utilitarian cousins. An uncommon structural system, yet similar to that at the Licorne Stadium, provides longitudinal resistance. Concerns about the humid corrosive environment and potential aesthetic distractions led to roof-plane moment-resisting frames substituting for the more conventional diagonal cross-bracing usually associated with portal frame construction.

Walls

The wall is another structural system capable of participating in the integration of architectural and structural forms. As exemplified by the

▲ **3.22**   Faculty of Journalism, Pamplona, Spain, Vicens and Ramos, 1996. Walls visually dominate the exterior.

▲ **3.23**   An interior architecture of walls.

Faculty of Journalism, Pamplona, walls not only dominate its façades, but also define interior spaces (Figs 3.22 and 3.23). In some areas of the building horizontal slots force the walls to span horizontally and function structurally like beams, and even balustrades read as low walls. Inside and out, walls dominate the architectural experience. Fortunately, any possible blandness arising from this architecture of walls is mitigated by exterior elevational and interior spatial variation, careful attention to surface textures, and the lightening of the concrete colour. The rectilinear form of the walls strengthens the orthogonal architecture they support, enclose and subdivide.

▲ **3.24** Casa del Fascio, Como, Italy, Giuseppe Terragni, 1936. Rational composition of frames and walls.

▲ **3.25** The central hall wrapped by frames.

This section concludes by observing how a combination of walls and frames can also synthesize architectural and structural form. In the Casa del Fascio, Como, widely acknowledged as Italy's most notable contribution to the Modern Movement, architectural and structural forms coalesce. Orthogonal frames, supplemented by several walls that provide lateral stability, order and structure a building square in plan with rectilinear façades. The expression of frames and walls is most overt on the front elevation (Fig. 3.24). The frames, and the walls to a lesser extent, organize interior space somewhat less rigidly than expected. As Blundell-Jones explains, the structural grid spacing varies subtly in several locations – to accommodate a large meeting room, to create more office depth and to reduce corridor width adjacent to the central gathering space.[10] The frames generally define room width and depth as well as circulation areas (Fig. 3.25). The Casa del Fascio, an epitome of orthogonality and rationality, is structured physically and conceptually by both walls and frames.

CONSONANT FORMS

Most buildings fall into this category where the architectural and structural forms neither synthesize, nor as discussed in the following section, contrast. Rather, a comfortable and usually unremarkable relationship exists between them. Often several different structural systems co-exist within the same architectural form. For example, frames and cross-bracing might resist gravity and lateral loads respectively. The following case studies illustrate several such buildings. Although their forms cannot be considered synthesized, they are nonetheless highly integrated. The buildings are discussed in a sequence that progresses from simple to more irregular architectural forms.

▲ **3.26** Mont-Cenis Academy, Herne, Germany, Jourda & Perraudin, 1999. A glazed box with an entry canopy.

▲ **3.27** Interior timber structure.

A glazed box encloses the Mont-Cenis Academy complex, a government training centre at Herne. An extended roof plane forms an entry canopy (Fig. 3.26). The self-contained campus includes three-storey accommodation blocks, library, administration, teaching spaces, dining rooms and spacious 'outdoor' areas. Responding to the site's coal mining history, a particularly environmentally friendly design approach is evidenced by the timber structure and the 'clouds' of photovoltaic cells that cover 50 per cent of the roof surface. A forest of poles supports continuous transverse timber trusses that in turn support composite timber and steel purlins. The vertical timber trusses that support the wall glazing provide face-load support for the walls, which exceed four storeys. Steel tension-only bracing in several bays within the perimeter walls and the roof plane ensures overall stability and wind resistance.

The visually dominant timber post-and-beam system with its regular grid layout, relates better to the architectural form than do the structural details. The roundness of the natural poles and the presence of the diagonal members in the roof and the wall-mullion trusses introduce non-orthogonal elements into an otherwise entirely rectilinear enclosure (Fig. 3.27). The diagonal steel rod cross-bracing in the roof plane and on the wall elevations also is at odds with the stark architectural form, but its fineness renders it barely discernible against the density of considerably larger timber members. An intriguing aspect about this project is the disparity of construction materials. Round timber poles, with little finishing other than bark removal, contrast strongly with the sleek glazed skin to highlight the differences between natural and artificial environments which lie at the heart of this project.

From the perspective of its architectural form, the European Institute of Health and Medical Sciences building, Guildford, represents a higher level of complexity. While in plan the building approximates a triangle

▲ **3.28**   European Institute of Health and Medical Sciences, Guildford, England, Nicholas Grimshaw & Partners Ltd, 1999. The prow rises above the main entrance.

▲ **3.29**   The curved roof structure.

with a rounded apex, in elevation the area above the main entry rises like a blunted ship's prow (Fig. 3.28). The roundedness of the prow in plan also appears in section at the roof level where a curved eaves area softens the architectural form. Several materials and systems constitute the structure. Vertical reinforced concrete walls concentrate in the front and rear plan areas and provide lateral stability, and columns elsewhere in plan support the weight of up to five flat-slab suspended floors. Inclined columns follow the building envelope profile to prop the cantilevering prow. Curved glue-laminated portal frames in the top floor achieve the exterior roundness of the roof form, and inside they strengthen the maritime metaphor implied by the architectural form (Fig. 3.29).

Similar curved timber members play a more extensive form-generating role in the two-storey Tobias Grau office and warehouse facility, Rellingen (Fig. 3.30). They wrap around the whole building, beginning from their connections above the ground floor slab, to define the ovoid-shaped envelope. The curved rafters are placed inside the metal roof but where they become columns they are exposed outside the skin of most walls where they support external glass louvres. Although the timber structure is the form-giver, most of the load-bearing structure is reinforced concrete. A first floor reinforced concrete flat-plate overlays a rectangular grid of reinforced concrete columns and several internal concrete walls provide lateral stability. Structure therefore comprises two different materials and three distinctly different structural systems, excluding the longitudinal steel cross-bracing at first floor level. Of all these systems only the curved timber portal frames relate closely to the tubular architectural form.

At the Pequot Museum, Mashantucket, Connecticut, the Gathering Space, the principal public area, takes a curved form in plan. Its spiralling

▲ **3.30** Tobias Grau headquarters, Rellingen, Germany, BRT Architekten, 1998. Glue-laminated ribs enclose the ground floor interior concrete structure.

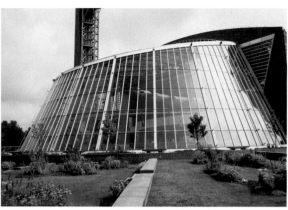

▲ **3.31** Pequot Museum, Mashantucket, USA, Polshek Partnership Architects, 2000. Exterior view of the Gathering Space.

▲ **3.32** The horizontal arch supports the curved and sloping wall.

geometry recalls that of fortified Pequot villages whose palisades were laid out as two offset semi-circles, and its curves also evoke the forms of Pequot wigwams, rounded in both plan and section. The north-facing Gathering Space is equivalent to a three- to four-storey volume (Fig. 3.31). Its semi-circular wall is glazed and radiating roof beams that slope away from the centre of the space are supported on inclined perimeter steel posts. Their cross-sectional dimensions have been minimized by the introduction of a most unexpected structural system – a horizontal arch, but one that synthesizes with the architectural form (Fig. 3.32).

▲ **3.33**   Säntispark Health and Leisure Centre, St Gallen, Switzerland, Raush, Ladner, Clerici, 1986. Creased and sagging roof.

Wind load acting at a right angle to the line of glazing over the centre half of the posts is resisted primarily by a semi-circular horizontal tube, anchored at each end. It functions either as an arch that works in compression, or as half a tension ring, depending on the wind direction. The arch, together with its stabilizing ties and connecting members back to the steel posts, adds another layer of structure that contributes complexity and interest to the interior space. An alternative to the steel tubular arch might have been to significantly increase the depth of the posts so they could span the whole height of the wall.

The roundedness of Pequot vernacular construction also finds expression in the roof structure. First, a bowstring truss spans the Gathering Space to support the radiating roof beams, and secondly, the two truss bottom-chords are curved in plan. Structural form is therefore very well integrated with architectural form which itself draws upon indigenous construction forms.

The following three examples illustrate consonant architectural and structural forms in the context of irregular architectural forms. When viewed from outside, the Säntispark Health and Leisure Centre, St Gallen, appears to have been distorted after construction. Was it originally configured differently in plan but then somehow moulded into its final curved and rounded forms, wrinkling and creasing the roof in the process (Fig. 3.33)? The ground floor plan and structural layout respond to the building form and function (Fig. 3.34). An essentially regular

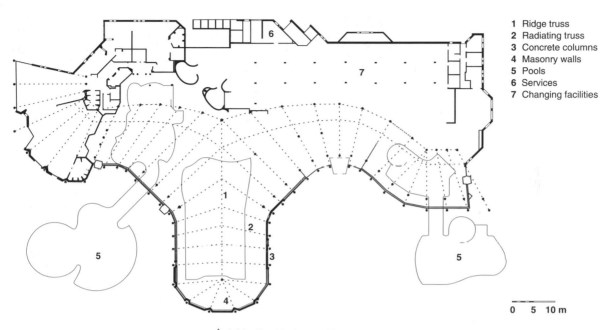

1 Ridge truss
2 Radiating truss
3 Concrete columns
4 Masonry walls
5 Pools
6 Services
7 Changing facilities

0   5   10 m

▲ **3.34** Simplified ground floor plan.

structural grid in the changing rooms and ancillary spaces dissipates in the recreational and pools areas. Here, any grid-like influence vanishes leaving structure to follow the informal organic geometry. It is as if the designers considered a rectilinear grid antithetical to a recreational environment. Uneven exterior column spacing reflects the 'elongations' and 'compressions' that occurred during the building plan 'distortion'. Columns define a curving perimeter envelope which in turn suggests the plan orientation of the roof trusses. They are generally positioned normal to the perimeter walls, except over the main pool where secondary trusses deliberately avoid forming a rectangular grid. In plan each truss is straight, but an obvious sag acknowledges its informal architectural setting (Fig. 3.35). Within an irregular form two structural materials and numerous structural systems combine to form a coherent and attractive work of architecture.

Irregularity of architectural form is not synonymous with curved forms. Consider the complex origami-inspired form of the Serpentine Gallery Pavilion 2001, London, also known as 'Eighteen Turns' (Fig. 3.36). Designed as a temporary building and constructed from planar sheets and ribbed elements, it was dismantled after the summer months of 2001 and relocated. The superstructure, excluding timber flooring, is fabricated entirely from aluminium – both structure and cladding. Ribs

▲ **3.35** Roof structure over main pool.

▲ **3.36** Eighteen Turns, Serpentine Gallery Pavilion 2001, London, England, Studio Libeskind Angular and planar surfaces.

▲ **3.37** Interior ribbed surfaces.

▲ **3.38** Verbier Sports Centre, Switzerland, André Zufferey, 1984. Complex stepping roof form.

form a post-and-beam structural system while the sheet cladding functions as shear walls, providing bracing for lateral loads. The orientation of the exposed interior ribs emphasizes each panel's non-orthogonal geometry (Fig. 3.37). The exposed structure enhances the shape and sense of panel directionality and intensifies the chaotic qualities of the assemblage. If a stressed skin or solid panel construction had been used its planar aesthetic would place this work into the category of synthesized forms.

The Verbier Sports Centre is the final example of consonant architectural and structural forms. The multiple pitched-roof form suits its surroundings. Roof planes step down to follow the mountainside slope and relate comfortably to the adjacent chalet pitched-roofs. Roof trusses run parallel to the slope and are articulated on the exterior where they bear on exposed concrete buttresses (Fig. 3.38). The stepping roof

▲ **3.39**   Visually complex roof structure over the pool.

▲ **3.40**   Exchange House, London, England, Skidmore, Owings & Merrill, 1993. Arches enable the building to span the site.

profile increases the truss complexity and reduces structural efficiency. Relatively large truss member sizes are required even though they are designed for heavy snow loads (Fig. 3.39). Although a lack of structural hierarchy among the many structural members obscures the primary structural form, a combination of timber's warm natural colour, unobtrusive timber connections and the filtering of natural light by the structure, contribute towards memorable architecture.

CONTRASTING FORMS

Architectural and structural forms contrast where a juxtaposition of architectural qualities such as geometry, materiality, scale and texture are observed. In the examples that follow, geometric dissimilarity between forms is the most common quality contrasted. At Exchange House, London, parabolic arches support a building rectilinear in plan and elevation (Fig. 3.40). The contrast between forms arises primarily from the need for the building to bridge underground railway lines, but even the exposed transverse cross-braced bays at each end of the building are unrelated to the architectural form (Fig. 3.41).

An element of surprise is also a feature common to buildings with contrasting forms. As one approaches a building and becomes aware of its architectural form one usually expects to discover a certain structural form based on one's previous architectural experience. If the actual form is considerably different from what is anticipated then it is likely that architectural and structural forms contrast.

Well-designed contrasting forms provide many opportunities for innovative and interesting architecture. Most examples of contrasting forms can be attributed to designers attempting to enliven their work, but

▲ **3.41**   A transverse exterior cross-braced frame.

▲ **3.42**   Fleet Place House, London, England, Skidmore, Owings & Merrill, 2000. Angled columns add interest to the main façade.

▲ **3.43**   Stuttgart Airport Terminal, Germany, von Gerkan • Marg + Partner, 1991. Structural 'trees'.

occasionally reasons arise from pragmatic considerations. Exchange House, for example, has to literally span its site due to subterranean features – and at Fleet Place House, London (Fig. 3.42), angled columns are not intended to inject interest into an otherwise repetitive commercial building façade, but to reduce construction costs by locating new columns over pre-existing foundations.[11]

Contrasting forms at Stuttgart Airport enrich its architecture and surprise building visitors in two ways. First, the structural geometry of the interior is totally unrelated to that of the enveloping form. Secondly, the meanings inherent in each form are so divergent – an interior structure that exudes meaning by virtue of its representational nature contrasts with the plain architectural form, essentially a truncated wedge. The monoslope roof rises from two to four storeys from land-side to air-side. Glazed roof slots subdivide the roof plane into twelve rectangular modules, each of which is supported by a completely unexpected structure in the form of a structural tree (Fig. 3.43). The 'trees', all the same height, bear on floors that step-up, one storey at a time. 'Trunks' consist of four interconnected parallel steel tubes which bend to become 'boughs' and then fork into clusters of three and four progressively smaller 'branches'. Finally, forty-eight 'twigs' support an orthogonal grid of rafters. Each 'tree canopy' covers an area of 22 m by 32 m, and contributes towards a unique and interesting interior space.

The architectural form of the Lille TGV Station is similar to that of the Stuttgart Airport Terminal. In cross-section the TGV Station floors also step-up two storeys across the site, but the roof shape, although approximating a monoslope, profiles as a gentle undulation (Fig. 3.44). What interior structure might be expected? Roof beams or trusses

▲ **3.44**   TGV Station, Lille, France, SNCF/Jean-Marie Duthilleul, 1994. Side elevation.

▲ **3.45**   Stazione Termini, Rome, Italy, Montuori, Vitellozzi, Calini, Castellazzi, Fatigati & Pintonello, 1950. Curved roof beams over the main concourse.

▲ **3.46**   Unexpected interior arches in the TGV Station.

following the roof profile like those at the Stazione Termini, Rome (Fig. 3.45), or like those at the better known Kansai Airport Terminal, by Renzo Piano? What is actually encountered is a series of paired steel arches that do not even follow the cross-sectional profile closely (Fig. 3.46). Disparities between the arch profiles and the roof wave are accounted for by vertical props that support secondary trusses directly under the roof. Because the prop diameters are similar to those of the primary arches, no clear structural hierarchy is established. Consequently an opportunity for the interior space to be characterized by a visual flow of arches is lost. Nevertheless, the combination of slender compression members and a filigree of stabilizing cables represents the designers' attempt to realize a vision of a roof structure with as few

▲ **3.47**   Hôtel du Département, Marseilles, France, Alsop & Störmer, 1994. Office block behind the Delibératif.

structural supports as possible and an appearance of 'fine lace floating above the train'.[12]

Contrasting geometries between architectural and structural forms, and even between structural forms within the same building, are evident at the Hôtel du Département (Regional Government Centre), Marseilles (Fig. 3.47). The project can be read as an amalgamation of at least four distinct architectural forms – two slab office-blocks linked by a transparent atrium, and two exterior elongated tubular forms. One, the Delibératif or council chambers, is free-standing while the Presidential offices sit above the higher office block.

The most obvious contrast between forms occurs within the first three storeys of the office blocks where exposed three-storey X-columns align longitudinally along each side. They visually dominate the lower storeys, both on the exterior where they are painted blue, and in the atrium where they are white. One reviewer describes them thus: 'the X-shaped concrete *pilotis* line up one after each other, their unexpected geometries ricocheting through the glazed atrium like sculptures by Barbara Hepworth, Frank Stella or the Flintstones'.[13] While their structural form does not relate to any other architectural qualities within the project, they function as transfer structures for gravity loads. They support columns located on a 5.4 m office module at third floor level and above and extend to a 10.8 m grid at ground floor level that is suitably large for basement car parking beneath. The architects deliberately expose the dramatic X-columns on the exterior by moving the building

▲ **3.48**   The Mediatéque 'hovers' and expresses instability in the atrium.

▲ **3.49**   Schools of Geography and Engineering, Marne-la-Vallée, Paris, France, Chaix & Morel, 1996. Vault-like roofs between blocks.

envelope into the building, behind the structure. Unexpected and spectacular, structure enriches both the interior space and the building exterior.

Upon entering the atrium, one discovers a third 'tube', the Mediatéque. Compared to the supporting structures of the Deliberatif and the Presidential offices, which due to either splaying or tapering legs appear very stable, the clusters of props under the Mediatéque suggest instability due to the way they converge towards a point at floor level (Fig. 3.48). It seems that unequal floor loading could cause the tube to topple. Only the relatively large diameters of the props themselves and their considerable bending strength avert such a catastrophe. So, within the space of a few metres where the giant X-columns ground and strongly brace the building, a quite different structural form is encountered that speaks of fragility and creates an impression of the Mediatéque 'hovering' or at least resting very lightly on its supports.

The new Schools of Geography and Engineering complex, Paris, also incorporates contrasting architectural and structural forms (Fig. 3.49). Three parallel rectilinear blocks are separated by courtyards partially enclosed by curved vault-like forms. While the main blocks are structured with conventional reinforced concrete walls and frames, the curved infill forms do not rely, as one might expect, on arches, but on an elaborate tension system. Their roof curvature follows concave catenary cables tied down at each end to foundations and pulled upwards at eight points along their lengths by tension rods hanging from the main blocks (Fig. 3.50). The fineness of the cables and rods contribute to achieving that often sought-after impression of 'floating' (Fig. 3.51).

This unusual structural system plays a significant pedagogical role in the school life, illustrating principles of structural mechanics to generations

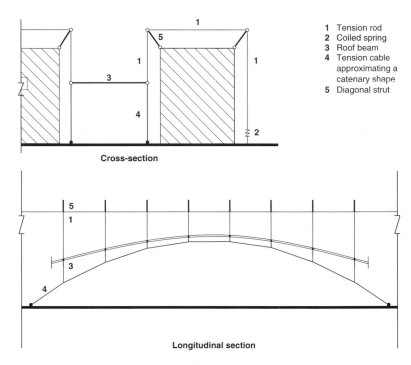

1	Tension rod
2	Coiled spring
3	Roof beam
4	Tension cable approximating a catenary shape
5	Diagonal strut

Cross-section

Longitudinal section

▲ **3.50** Diagrammatic representation of the curved-roof support structure.

▲ **3.51** Curved 'floating' roof.

▲ **3.52** Exterior tension rods and springs.

▲ **3.53** Stealth Building, Culver City, USA, Eric Owen Moss Architects, 2001. Triangular form at the northern end.

of civil engineering students. Vertical steel rods at regular centres support the curved roof. They hang from projecting diagonal compression struts that are tied to identical struts on the other side of the higher rectilinear block roofs by horizontal rods. On the far sides of the two end rectilinear blocks, horizontal rod tensions are resolved by vertical rods that connect to large coil tension-springs tied to the foundations (Fig. 3.52).

While the curved roof is pulled upwards by this sprung tensioned system, its catenary cables are tensioned down to a different set of springs and foundations. The roof therefore hovers, simultaneously held in space by opposing tension forces – totally reliant upon the tensioned ties for its equilibrium. In these buildings contrast occurs not only between the linear and curved architectural forms, and vaulted forms reliant on tension rather than on compression, but also between the innovative tensioned roof system and the conventional reinforced concrete framing elsewhere. One form is clearly 'grounded' and the other 'floats', although securely tethered to the ground.

Contrasting architectural and structural forms are also evident at the geometrically challenging Stealth Building, Los Angeles. For a start the architectural form itself transforms along the building's length – from a triangular cross-section at the northern end to a conventional rectilinear shape at the south (Fig. 3.53). While the moment-resisting frames that structure the southern end relate closely to the reasonably rectilinear form of that area, the structure elsewhere responds to other issues. For example, at the north end, four columns support two longitudinal trusses that carry the second floor, the mezzanine and the roof. These trusses enable the building to span over an outdoor sunken theatre and maintain the proscenium arch opening through its rear wall into the building behind. Making up the third structural system, in the central area which accommodates vertical circulation and bathrooms, steel tubes on an axis angled to the main structural axes support cantilevered triangulation to which light-weight eaves and balcony construction is attached.

Apart from these structural elements, structure maintains an orthogonality that flies in the face of the angled lines and the sloping planar surfaces of the building enclosure. Floor plate geometry does not follow the lines of structural support but rather ignores the generally rational structural layout to satisfy the goal of completing the global geometrical transformation. As described by the architect: 'The aspiration is to investigate a changing exterior form and a varying interior space; to construct a building whose constant is constantly moving, re-making both outside and inside . . .'[14] Structure and construction clash, but both systems maintain their integrity and independence (Fig. 3.54).

All the previous examples in this section are drawn from relatively new buildings completed in and around the 1990s. Contrasting architectural and structural forms are part of their original designs. Yet we commonly

▲ **3.54** An interior office space where the sloping wall angles across the line of the truss.

encounter other examples of contrasting forms in additions or modifications to existing buildings, particularly given significant age differences between the old and new work.

The Reichstag cupola, discussed previously, is one of many such examples reviewed by Byard.[15] While architectural and structural forms synthesize in the cupola itself, both contrast with those of the original building. A similar situation arises at the Great Court of the British Museum, London. A new canopy covers an irregularly shaped space between the circular Reading Room and numerous neo-classical load-bearing wall buildings surrounding the courtyard (Fig. 3.55). The canopy, a triangulated steel surface structure, differs dramatically from the buildings it spans between. Greater differences in architectural and structural forms, materiality, and degrees of lightness and transparency are hardly possible.

As expected, the canopy has attracted considerable comment. Reviewers generally admire it. They point to its design and construction complexity, its controlled day-lighting, and note its elegance, describing it as 'floating', 'delicate', and 'unobtrusive', at least when compared to an original scheme with heavier orthogonal structure and reduced transparency. However, its billowing form is easier to comprehend from above than from within, where one experiences a visual restlessness from the continuous triangulation of the doubly-curved surfaces. An

▲ **3.55** The Great Court, British Museum, London, England, Foster and Partners, 2000. Triangulated lattice roof with the circular Reading Room on the left.

absence of structural hierarchy contributes to this reduction of spatial and structural comprehension, further highlighting the contrast between the new and the old.

SUMMARY

In order to discuss the relationships between architectural and structural form an understanding of the term *architectural form* is intentionally narrowly defined as the massing or the enveloping form. The reality of most architectural design practice is that structure rarely generates architectural form, but rather responds to it in a way that meets the programme and ideally is consistent with design concepts. Selected buildings illustrate three categories of relationship between architectural and structural form – synthesis, consonance and contrast. No one category or attitude to the relationship between forms is inherently preferable to another. The examples provided merely hint at the breadth of potential similarity or diversity of forms that can lead to exemplary architecture.

REFERENCES AND NOTES

1   Ching, F. D. (1996). *Architecture: Form-Space and Order*, 2nd edn. Van Nostrand Reinhold.

2   Suckle, A. (1980). *By Their Own Design*. Whitney Library of Design.

3   Quoted by Suckle (1980), p. 14.

4   Quoted in Collins, P. (1998). *Changing Ideals in Modern Architecture 1750–1950*, 2nd edn. McGill–Queen's University Press, p. 214.

5   Nervi, P. L. (1955). Concrete and structural form. *The Architect and Building News*, 208 (27), pp. 523–9.

6   Glasser, D. E. (1979). Structural considerations. In J. Synder and A. Catanse (eds), *Introduction to Architecture*. McGraw–Hill, pp. 268–71.

7   For other examples see J. Chilton (2000). *The Engineer's Contribution to Contemporary Architecture: Heinz Isler*. RIBA Telford.

8   Condit, C. W. (1964). *The Chicago School of Architecture*. The University of Chicago Press, p. 90.

9   Thiel-Siling, S. (ed.) (1998). *Icons of Architecture: the 20th Century*. Prestel, p. 125.

10 Blundell-Jones, P. (2002). *Modern Architecture Through Case-Studies*. Architectural Press, p. 153.

11 Bussel, A. (2000). *SOM evolutions: Recent Work of Skidmore, Owings & Merrill*. Birkhäuser.

12 Quoted by Davey, P. (1996). In The boot and the lace maker. *Architectural Review*, 199 (3), p. 72.

13 Welsh, J. (1994). Willing and able. *RIBA Journal*, April, pp. 37–47.

14 Moss, E. O. (2000). Eric Owen Moss: the Stealth. *GA Document*, 61, pp. 60–62.

15 Byard, P. S. (1998). *The Architecture of Additions: Design and Regulation*. W. W. Norton & Company.

4 BUILDING EXTERIOR

INTRODUCTION

In many urban locations site boundaries and recession planes determine architectural form. Particularly for medium- to high-rise buildings, economic and pragmatic necessity give rise to ubiquitous rectilinear forms that require architectural approaches other than the manipulation of building massing for them to contribute positively to the urban fabric. With the exception of those buildings completely clad in mirror glass or some other type of opaque cladding, many buildings world-wide share the common feature of some exposed structural elements on their façades. Arising more from an appreciation of the functional advantages perimeter structure affords, than intentionally exposing structure for its own sake, structural members are often exposed. While such structural ordering and patterning of façades often merely reflects that of the surrounding built environment and therefore tends to proliferate architecture of indifferent quality, some architects take a more proactive stance towards exposing structure. They are aware of its potential to enrich exterior architecture.

Before considering in breadth the diverse contributions that structure brings to building exteriors, the chapter begins by examining one building more deeply, the Hong Kong and Shanghai Bank, Hong Kong. A study of the exposed structure on its main façade sets the scene for discussing many of the roles exterior structure plays that this chapter explores.

▲ **4.1** Hong Kong and Shanghai Bank, Hong Kong, China, Foster and Associates, 1986. Main façade.

One of the bank's most distinctive features is its exposed structure on the main façade (Fig. 4.1). If this structure were to be concealed behind cladding, one of the world's best-known commercial buildings would no longer be recognizable. Devoid of its iconic structure it would merely merge with its neighbours' more conventional architecture.

Development of the unusual structural form arose primarily from the client's insistence on retaining an existing historic banking chamber that occupied the side. Foster and Associates' first sketches for the competition to select an architect show large exposed bridge-like trusses spanning across the building and supporting suspended floors beneath.[1] After being commissioned, the architects continued to develop long-span structural schemes. Although the client eventually decided to trim the budget and demolish the banking chamber, commitment to a long-span structural solution was justified by studies that showed large column-free areas yielded significantly higher rental returns than shorter-span options. The client also appreciated the high level of planning flexibility that long spans provided. After abandoning the relatively crude bridge-truss design, a series of structural iterations that always included strongly exposed structure were continually refined until the final structural scheme emerged.

So, how does structure contribute to the exterior architecture of the bank? Beginning with its visual qualities, one notes how the structure is located in front of the cladding. Separated from the façade, structure modulates it, providing depth, pattern and order. The vertical structure, namely three hanger-rods and two ladder-like masts, create a symmetrical and rhythmical ababa composition. On a macro scale, the horizontal trusses subdivide the façade vertically, while beams within the ladder frames that can also be described as vierendeel masts, articulate individual storey heights at a finer scale. From a distance, structural scale relates well to the overall building scale. Structure, clearly distinguished from other building elements such as cladding, can be read clearly as such, yet a sense of structural monumentality is avoided. To my eye at least, structural scale verges on the minimal, even without allowing for the thickness of protective layers of cladding that encase the steelwork. However, close up, and especially inside the building, those apparently slender façade structural members appear huge. An interior column located within a single-storey space exerts an overwhelming presence due to its relatively large scale in such a confined volume.

As well as structure's contribution to the visual composition of the façade and the way its exposure links the interior and exterior architecture, structure can also be read as playing several expressive roles – such as expressing structural actions, building function and conceptual issues. The triangulated geometry of the double coat-hanger trusses shows how they transfer loads from their mid-spans and end tension-hangers to the vierendeel masts. At a more detailed level though, the expression of structural actions is somewhat inconsistent. While the increasing diameter of the tension-hangers towards the underside of each truss accurately reflects the accumulative increase of weight from the suspended floors, the enlargements at the ends of truss members suggest rigid connectivity rather than the reality of large structural pin joints. At a functional level, the mega-frame subdivides the façade to reflect functional and organizational aspects within the building. Masts separate service areas from the main banking hall and offices, and vertical spacing between trusses expresses five broadly separate functional divisions within the bank. Overlaying this functional expression, exposed structure articulates the High-Tech and state-of-the-art qualities of design and construction.

The following section of this chapter examines the aesthetic quality of exterior structure in more detail. Then, after illustrating how architects use structure to create strong visual connections between exterior and interior architecture, the chapter considers the relationship of exterior structure to building entry. Finally, it concludes by exploring the expressive roles played by exterior structure.

AESTHETIC QUALITIES

The exterior character of a building is often determined by how structure relates to the building envelope. Architects frequently explore and exploit spatial relationships between these two elements in order to express their architectural ideas and generally enrich their designs.[2] Structure plays numerous roles in contributing to the visual appearance of a building façade, through modulation, adding depth and texture, and acting as a visual screen or filter. Some of these roles are seen at the Hong Kong and Shanghai Bank. In all of them the structural scale must relate appropriately to the scales of the surrounding elements in order to achieve the desired outcome.

Modulation

Where beams and columns modulate a façade, they usually visually subdivide the skin vertically and horizontally, creating a rectangular ordering pattern over the building surface. Within these structural modules, secondary structural members, perhaps supporting glazing and themselves an order of magnitude smaller than the primary structural modulators, may further subdivide the surfaces.

Modulation generates patterns that potentially introduce variety, rhythm and hierarchy, and generally increases visual interest. Patterned or textured surfaces are usually preferable to those that are planar and bare. However, as seen on many office building façades, if the modulation is too repetitious it ceases to be an attractive architectural feature. Given its ubiquitous nature, modulation hardly requires illustration, but five rather unusual examples are discussed.

In response to its beach-front marine environment and an architectural concept centred on the beaching of crystalline rocks, a glazed envelope encloses the Kursaal auditorium perimeter structure at San Sebastian. Although not exposed, structure is visible, albeit dimly. The deep external wall structure that rises over 20 m to the roof is sandwiched between two skins of translucent glass panels. Structural framing that takes the

▲ **4.2**   Kursaal Auditorium and Conference Centre, San Sebastian, Spain, Rafael Moneo, 1999. Structure behind translucent glazed panels modulates exterior walls.

form of vertical or slightly inclined vierendeel trusses that are tied together by regularly spaced horizontal members is therefore perceived as shadowy forms from both inside and out (Fig. 4.2). Although considerably subdued visually, structure still modulates the large exterior and interior wall surfaces, and on the side walls its geometrical distortions accentuate the building's subtle inclination towards the sea.

A more typical example of structure modulating a whole façade can be observed at the Yerba Buena Lofts, San Francisco (Fig. 4.3). Visually dominant primary structural elements – walls and slabs, play two roles simultaneously. While modulating and ordering the façade they also alter one's perception of the building's scale. Concealment of the mezzanine floor structure behind glazing in each double-height apartment means the ten-storey building is read as five storeys. To prevent the repetitive structural elements becoming over-bearing, translucent textured glass cladding to half of each apartment combine with set-back glazed walls to form balconies and provide welcome depth to the façade. Four recesses in plan along the building length, including one at each end, introduce even more variety.

At 88 Wood Street, London, structure is selectively exposed – in this case at the base of the building. Perimeter columns are set back 1.5 m from the street frontage to reduce the span and structural depth of interior floor beams. By minimizing structural depth, the developers gained an extra storey height within a restricted building volume. On the upper floors, a floor-to-ceiling glazed skin extends in front of the structural grid,

▲ **4.3** Yerba Buena Lofts, San Francisco, USA, Stanley Saitowitz Office/Natoma Architects, 2002. Walls and slabs modulate the front façade.

▲ **4.4** 88 Wood Street, London, England, Richard Rogers Partnership, 2000. Columns introduce rhythm and modulation at ground floor level.

▲ **4.5** RAC Control Centre, Bristol, England, Nicholas Grimshaw & Partners, 1995. Structural piers modulate the base perimeter.

concealing it from the outside. The resulting double-height blind-colonnade that visually functions as a base to the building, runs along the Wood Street frontage until the skin moves further into the building to accommodate the steps and ramp to the main entrance (Fig. 4.4). At pavement level, due to their size and modest spacing, the columns contribute a strong sense of rhythm. In the evening, when down-lit, the concrete

▲ **4.8**   Cathédrale Nôtre Dame, Paris, France, 1260. Deep perimeter structure surrounds the chevet.

▲ **4.9**   Dulles International Airport, Washington, DC, USA, Saarinen (Eero) and Associates, 1962. Piers create deep bays along the façade.

with its architecture, and in particular its cathedrals, whose walls are flanked by massive exterior structure. Buttresses topped by pinnacles and supporting flying buttresses contribute an extraordinary depth and texture as a by-product of structural necessity (Fig. 4.8).

Modern structural systems usually do not require nearly as much depth, but architects often welcome whatever depth is available for the aesthetic value it brings to a building exterior. For example, deep perimeter structure juts out from Dulles International Airport terminal, Washington, DC. Unlike Gothic buttresses that resist compression thrusts originating from masonry roof vaults, the terminal's piers resist tension forces arising from a reinforced concrete catenary roof (see Fig. 3.10). The piers are very substantial even though an outward inclination reduces the bending moments they must resist. Their elegant taper reflects both structural actions and the architect's desire to express 'the movement and excitement of modern travel by air'.[4]

From most viewpoints the piers visually dominate the exterior of the terminal. They provide depth and rhythm to the front façade (Fig. 4.9). Even though fully glazed walls butt into the sides of piers and limit the extent of their exposure, by curving the glazed walls in-plan into the building, additional façade depth is gained. This masterful design move simultaneously dissipates the possible visual severity of planar outward-sloping surfaces, echoes the profile of the curved canopy above, and also accentuates both points of entry and bays between the piers for people to meet and wait in. The curved walls also allow for wind face-loads to be resisted by horizontal arch or catenary action depending on the wind direction, reducing considerably wall framing member dimensions and maximizing transparency.

Although designers usually provide structural depth to façades using ribbed or discrete elements, as in the previous example, continuous structure like an undulating wall presents other possibilities. If folded or curved in plan, the structural depth and the stability and strength normal to the plane of a wall increase. Such a wall can therefore be understood as a vertically cantilevered folded-plate when resisting face loads. In the context of this chapter, shaping a wall in plan presents opportunities for architectural enrichment, as illustrated at the Mönchengladbach Museum. Highly regarded for the qualities of its interior spaces and urban setting, an exterior gallery wall undulates (Fig. 4.10). The sinuous wall imbues one gallery interior with special character and outside, the wall's serpentine geometry appears as a natural extension of the curvilinear paths and brick walls that lead up the hillside to the museum. The gently curving wall possesses an attractive softness and naturalness.

No doubt the texture of brickwork also enhances one's enjoyment of this small section of the museum. Texture implies variation of surface depth and is linked to materiality. Each material possesses a unique texture depending on how it is fabricated, formed or finished. For example, before the introduction of metal arc welding the texture of steel-plated structural connections arose from overlapping plates and single or multiple rows of rivets. Since the advent of welding, plates can be butt-welded together and the weld ground flush, forming an almost invisible connection and reducing the surface texture. Other steel textures have not changed over time, especially the ribs and stiffening plate sections that prevent large areas of thin steel plate from buckling. At Mound Stand, London, this texture contributes significantly to the exterior surfaces (Fig. 4.11).

Due to the planning and construction constraints arising from placing a new stand over one already existing, some unusual structural solutions were called for. Along the rear and the side-walls of the stand, gravity loads are resisted and transferred to supporting members by one-storey-deep steel plate-girders. From a distance they appear as walls, but upon closer inspection one recognizes vertical and horizontal stiffening plates, the unmistakable language of thin steel-plate construction. This texture not only conveys a strong sense of materiality and speaks of the deep member's structural responsibilities, but it also enriches the surface qualities of the building, better known for its tension-membrane roof structure.

Structural texture is even more strongly associated with timber construction. Consider, for example, a traditional timber roof with its hierarchical construction. Beginning with primary members, say beams, successively shallower members like rafters and purlins and then sarking progressively build up the structural depth as they overlay each other at right-angles.

With a structural form far more sophisticated than for most timber structures, the World Exhibition Centre Canopy, Hanover, also possesses a much admired hierarchical structural texture. Although the main members, the masts and cantilevering ribs are themselves textured, the fine ribbed-shell structure spanning between the cantilevers and covered by a timber lattice and a white water-proof membrane appeals to the eye (Fig. 4.12).

Screening and filtering

Depending on its depth, density in plan and elevation, and its spatial relationship to a building envelope, exterior structure can be read as a screen or filter, contributing yet another set of aesthetic qualities to a façade.

▲ **4.10** Mönchengladbach Museum, Germany, Hans Hollein, 1982. Curved exterior gallery walls respond to the site contours.

▲ **4.11** Mound Stand, Lord's Cricket Ground, London, England, Michael Hopkins & Partners, 1987. Horizontal and vertical stiffening plates texture a steel beam-wall along the rear of the stand just below the tension-membrane roof.

▲ **4.12** Canopy structure, World Exhibition Centre, Hanover, Germany, Herzog + Partner, 1999. Attractive textured soffit surfaces.

▲ **4.13** Exhibition Centre, Melbourne, Australia, Denton Corker Marshall, 1996. Verandah posts visually soften the façade.

▲ **4.14** A view along the verandah.

The main façade of the Melbourne Exhibition Centre that faces the Yarra River illustrates clearly how exterior structure screens and filters. A multitude of slender steel posts on a close 3 m by 3 m grid support a wide verandah that slopes away from the main building (Fig. 4.13). The posts, two bays deep, tilt away from the building to maintain orthogonality with the verandah roof. Their rotation from the vertical introduces a sense of movement that explains why, when viewed from a distance, the posts are likened to reeds along a riverbank. From that same view, it is difficult to discern the building envelope beyond them. It fades into the background behind the sheer numbers of posts that screen and soften it. From inside the Centre, one appreciates the extent to which the posts diffuse natural light and filter views toward the river. A promenade along the building edge through the posts yields a final delight – their slenderness, close spacing and uniform tilt recalls walking through saplings of a windblown forest (Fig. 4.14).

At Library Square, Vancouver, an exterior structural frame curves around the main rectilinear library block, wrapping and screening it (Fig. 4.15). In two locations, where the frame almost touches corners of the library, gaps open in the frame, allowing glimpses of the library behind. Appearing as trabeated construction longitudinally and vaulted construction transversely, the frame's single-bay deep structure explicitly references the Colosseum in Rome. An open and arcaded ground floor structure repeats at roof level as an open framework and floors at other levels accommodate reading galleries. The openness of the framework provides plenty of natural light for perimeter reading areas and filters light entering the main library.

▲ **4.15** Library Square, Vancouver, Canada, Moshe Safdie and Associates Inc., 1995. A gap reveals the cross-section of the screening frame and a glimpse of the main library block behind.

▲ **4.16** Getty Center, Los Angeles, USA, Richard Meier & Partners, 1997. Exterior structure deepens the rear of the Rotunda.

▲ **4.17** A colonnade supporting an elevated walkway alongside an external wall.

While less overt at the Getty Center, Los Angeles, structural elements play important screening roles in many locations around the museum complex. In some cases by varying the relative positions of structure and skin in plan, structure projects beyond the building enclosure to contribute depth and to some extent screen the façades. This strategy can be observed where the Rotunda backs onto the Museum Courtyard (Fig. 4.16). The exterior columns of many buildings are exposed and act as counterpoints to adjacent walls. In other areas, exterior colonnades that support canopies or walkways enrich the experience of walking beside the buildings (Fig. 4.17). This layering of structure in front of the façades deepens them and effectively screens them, successfully reducing the undesirable visual dominance of potentially large areas of bare wall.

Compared to the relatively deep structural screens at the Melbourne Exhibition Centre, Library Square, and to a lesser extent the Getty Center, most screening structure on the main façade of the Centre Pompidou, Paris, lies within a vertical plane (Fig. 4.18). Located in front of the building envelope a distance almost equal to the length of a ger-berette,[5] the screen consists of slender horizontal tubes and vertical and diagonal tension rods. The exterior structure, mainly resisting tension forces, is so fine it risks being misread as scaffolding. Although ineffective as a screen or filter for natural light, the large number of members and

▲ **4.18**   Centre Pompidou, Paris, France, Piano and Rogers, 1977. Screening effect of structure on the main façade.

▲ **4.19**   Mexican Embassy, Berlin, Germany, González de León and Serrano, 2000. Dynamic columned-walls.

their light colour create a fine mesh-like screen that lessens the visual impact of the exposed columns and wall cladding behind it. From a functional perspective, the horizontal separation of the screen from the envelope provides width for circulation routes along the front façade, and space for exposed services at the rear.

The main façade of the Mexican Embassy, Berlin, is the final example of exterior structure functioning as a screen (Fig. 4.19). Forty closely spaced and over-structured concrete mullions-cum-columns, necessitated by neither gravity nor wind loads, satisfy security and aesthetic requirements. By virtue of their depth and close spacing the columns achieve a reasonable degree of physical and visual security. Although pedestrians can see through the glass panes between columns when standing directly in front of them, from oblique angles the columned-wall becomes opaque.

The architects' goal 'to create a building that possessed an unmistakable image' necessitated a creative approach to configuring the façade.[6] Several subtle geometric manipulations of the 17 m high columns transform a potentially repetitive façade into one comprising two columned planes, both angled inwards and one warped to achieve a dynamic visual effect.

Beginning at the left-hand side of the embassy as seen from the street, vertical columns step back progressively from the pavement towards the entrance. To the right of the entrance, column bases lie on a straight-line between it and the corner of the building. However, the set-out line for the tops of the columns does not parallel the set-out line for their bases. From the right-hand corner of the building as seen from the street, the upper set-out line angles away from the column-base line below towards the street so that the top of the column closest to the entrance is located approximately 3 m in front of its base. This simple geometric variation between top and bottom set-out lines creates a warped surface, affecting the visual impact of the columns profoundly. As the eye moves relative to the columns, they also appear to move. An exquisite rough-chiseled finish to the white concrete columns completes the structure's positive visual contribution and reflects the embassy's high quality design and construction.

Structural scale

Structural scale strongly influences how exterior structure contributes aesthetically to a façade. The dimensions of structural members can lie anywhere on a continuum between the extremes of mesh-like fineness and massive monumentality. Several buildings, beginning with those utilizing small-scale structure, illustrate varied approaches to structural scale.

Where steel is used most efficiently, in tension, members invariably fall into the category of small scale – a consequence of sufficient strength gained from minimal cross-sectional area. At the Cathédrale Nôtre Dame de la Treille, Lille, a stainless steel rod-and-tube structure, reminiscent of a spider's web, supports a new exterior nave wall (Figs 4.20 and 4.21). This diaphanous steelwork contrasts with both the new post-tensioned stone arch needed to equilibrate the tension within the exposed steelwork, and the cathedral's original masonry structural elements. In this project, the dimensions of the exterior steel members were deliberately minimized by pre-tensioning the steel.[7] Shadows from large structural members

<figure>▲ 4.25   Stansted Airport terminal, Essex, England, Foster Associates, 1991. Portico 'trees' are an extension of the interior structure.</figure>

<figure>▲ 4.26   Mont-Cenis Academy, Herne, Germany, Jourda & Perraudin, 1999. The front canopy structure is almost identical to that of the interior.</figure>

to the interior structure and then letting those decisions in conjunction with other ideals like transparency, inform the exterior design. However, correspondence between exterior and interior structure may also have deeper roots. There may be a conscious reaction against the practice of façadism where a façade bears little relationship to the rest of the building, or a concern for a holistic and integrated architecture with a demonstrable relatedness between exterior and interior. An outside/inside connection need not be literal but might entail external expression of the interior structural qualities, rather than the exposure of actual members and details.

High-Tech architects usually make the interior/exterior connection explicit, as exemplified by the Hong Kong and Shanghai Bank. At Stansted Airport Terminal, Essex, also designed by Foster Associates, the structural 'trees' that dominate the terminal's interior extend from behind the glazed front wall to support a full-length portico (Fig. 4.25 and see Fig. 9.8).

The Mont-Cenis Academy, Herne (Figs 3.26 and 4.26) also gives similar advanced notice of its interior structure on the exterior. Timber posts and roof structure that support a full-width entrance canopy are a pure extension of the structure inside the building envelope. Although the exterior posts are as naturally detailed as all others, they have required slight structural modification. Due to the canopy roof span lengths being longer than elsewhere, steel rod composite-action has been added to supplement the vertical load-bearing capacity of the posts. This is not the only time composite-action appears in the building. It is similar to the system used throughout the roof structure to extend the span of the timber purlins without increasing their dimensions.

Clearly expressed composite timber and steel construction also connects exterior and interior at the Wilkhahn Factory, Bad Münder (Fig. 4.27). Here the choice of structural materials is well suited to the furniture-maker owner. The roof structure, comprising steel rods that greatly extend the structural capacity of the timber roof beams, spans between steel-braced timber masts. The structural system is repeated four times across the width of the building. Unfortunately, densely clustered hanging light-fittings limit the extent to which the interior structure can be appreciated.

In each of the buildings considered above, the whole interior structural system repeats on the exterior. A more subtle approach, perhaps suited to a wider range of architectural styles, entails the exposure of just one structural element that reflects the interior structural qualities of the building. Two large columns with haunched capitals that designate entry

▲ **4.27** Wilkhahn Factory, Bad Münder, Germany, Herzog with Bernd Steigerwald, 1993. Longitudinal structural form is exposed.

▲ **4.28** Public University of Navarra, Pamplona, Spain, Sáenzde Oiza Arquitectos, 1993. The pair of exterior columns are precursors to columnar interior architecture.

to the central block of the Public University of Navarra, Pamplona, exemplify this approach (Fig. 4.28). Without literally reproducing the interior columns they set the scene for an almost overwhelming display of columnar interior architecture. Their conical capitals, circular stems and concrete materiality make an unambiguous connection (see Fig. 5.16). At each end of the building, two levels of colonnades set within exterior walls connect to the interior structure even more explicitly.

▲ **4.29**   Millennium Stadium, Cardiff,
Wales, The Lobb Partnership (now HOK
Sports), 2000. Main entry is under the beam
between the mast legs.

ENTRY

Provision and articulation of entry, very important aspects of architectural design, provide endless opportunities for structural participation. At a basic level, structure might contribute little more than the support of an entry canopy. Yet in another building, structure might function as the architectural element that creates a sense of entry, its expression and celebration. The columns framing the main entrance to the Public University of Navarra above, fall into this category, and the following examples also illustrate structure playing significant roles in marking and defining entry. Each entrance's structural form is totally different, relating either to the structural layout of its own building, or in the final example, to that of its neighbouring structures.

Eighty-metre-high masts located at its four corners define the main entry points to the Millennium Stadium, Cardiff. Spectators enter under structural frames at the bases of the masts supporting outriggers that cantilever inside the stadium to carry the primary 220 m long roof trusses that retractable roof units move along (Fig. 4.29). The role of signifying entry, that canopies usually play, is amply fulfilled by structural elements. Multiple horizontal and inclined structural booms and ties project outwards in a grand welcoming gesture while the huge beam and mast legs above ground level articulate the entry area.

These impressive tubular-steel mast structures required significant design modifications in order to accommodate entry. The cross-bracing extending down the mast is interrupted above ground level by the deep beam. Together with the mast legs it forms a single-storey moment-resisting frame that avoids the need for ground level bracing and simultaneously creates an entry portal. The massiveness of this structural threshold appropriately prepares spectators for the huge enclosure that lies beyond it.

Structure also defines entry to the elevated departures area at Terminal 2F, Charles de Gaulle Airport, Paris (Figs 4.30 and 4.31). In this case, pedestrians enter between structural members rather than underneath them. The entrance locations along the building frontage correspond to the structural organization of the concourse roof – a system of paired primary steel ribs carrying secondary structure that supports the impressive concrete ceiling slabs. V-shaped struts project down from the ribs and bear upon greatly enlarged vertical concrete columns, semi-circular in cross-section. The column orientation and its form suggest a dramatic reading. An original single circular column appears to have been split in half and both halves then moved apart to create an entrance.

▲ **4.30**   Charles de Gaulle Airport: Terminal 2F, Paris, France, Aéroports de Paris, 1999. Semi-circular columns signal entry.

▲ **4.31**   A 'split-column' viewed from inside.

Entry between these columns is particularly memorable. As seen from the footpath, the columns clearly signify entry by projecting outside the cladding line rhythmically in step with the roof structure. Although it seems perverse to enter through a massing of concrete when the whole wall cladding is otherwise glazed, upon entry one enjoys pondering the immense physical force required to 'split' and 'move' the concrete semi-circles apart. Given the apparent effort required for its construction the entrance therefore has special significance. After the experience of passing between the columns one discovers that their shapes and materiality complement other curved and exposed concrete surfaces throughout the terminal.

The pitched entrance canopy structure of the Dome Leisure Centre, Doncaster, also marks entry quite unambiguously and introduces visitors to the interior structure (Fig. 4.32). Inside the building, identical interior triangulated structure defines and modulates the pedestrian mall leading to the heart of the complex, the dome. Exterior structure is therefore an extension of the interior structure, displaying a structural language consistently spoken throughout the centre, namely, perforated steel I-sections and steel tubes.

Like the Terminal 2F entrances (Fig. 4.30), the Leisure Centre entry canopy is over-structured. While its visual severity arising from the use of large members is reduced by their generous circular penetrations and tapered sections that introduce additional liveliness, one wonders to what extent this grey-coloured structural display helps realize the architect's intent 'to embody the exuberant spirit of leisure'.[8] However, the structure certainly defines entry clearly, and an absence of orthogonality

▲ **4.32**   Dome Leisure Centre, Doncaster, England, FaulknerBrowns Architects, 1989. Structure articulates entry.

▲ **4.33**   Cité de la Musique, Paris, France, Christian de Portzamparc, 1995. Entrance structure.

with its connotations of formality no doubt encourages a more relaxed attitude in building visitors.

The Cité de la Musique, Paris, provides the final example of structure articulating entry. An open rectangular framework designates entry (Fig. 4.33). Its four closely spaced two-storey-plus red frames reference the nearby Parc de la Villette follies, less than a hundred metres away. Therefore, rather than reflecting interior structure which in this building is not particularly evident, the entrance responds to external influences. Unlike the open frameworks that inspired the canopy design, Portzamparc's entry folly bears load from two trusses forming an elongated wedge. The trusses, visible through the glazed walls of the wedge that defines a linear circulation spine, visually tie the entrance framework to the main building. Since the trusses bear on the first storey beams, the structural members above that level are essentially gestural. The open frames of the Cité de la Musique entry structure successfully fulfil common architectural expectations by marking entry and encouraging it.

EXPRESSIVE ROLES

Exterior structure has a long tradition of playing expressive roles. Consider Gothic cathedrals. Their pinnacles, flying-buttresses and buttresses express how the horizontal thrusts from masonry roof vaults are resisted and transferred to the ground (see Fig. 4.8). Load paths become legible through a combination of structural layout, shape and scale. On the other hand, Renaissance exterior structure, such as at S. Giorgio Maggiore, Venice, expresses aspects other than the Romanesque interior or its structural actions. Four giant attached-columns dominate the façade (Fig. 4.34). They appear to be supporting a section of pediment thrust up

▲ **4.34** S. Giorgio Maggiore, Venice, Italy, Palladio, 1610. The Classical façade does not relate to the Romanesque interior within.

from one that previously spanned the entire width of the church. Framing the main entrance, they express monumentality and the importance of the nave in relation to the aisles.

Contemporary exterior structure continues this expressive tradition by communicating a diverse range of ideas, architectural qualities and actions. Exterior structure can to some degree express any architectural idea. The clarity with which such an idea might be communicated is quite another matter. That certainly depends on an architect's skill. In the following four examples, structure expresses quite different ideas.

The exterior of Fitzwilliam College Chapel, Cambridge, differentiates itself from adjoining architectural forms to express ideas of protection and enclosure (Fig. 4.35). The chapel's distinctive circular geometry sets it apart from the surrounding rectilinear blocks. As an extension to a 1960s linear accommodation wing, the chapel adopts the same width as the existing construction where it connects. Then, after provision of a circulation area several metres long, perimeter walls begin to form a cylinder, increasing the building width and partially encircling the chapel inside. Like embracing arms, in an understated and simple manner, they protect and enclose, metaphorically as well as physically. As at the Mönchengladbach Museum (see Fig. 4.10), the act of curving walls in plan increases their strength and stability against horizontal loads. The

▲ **4.35** Fitzwilliam College Chapel, Cambridge, England, Richard MacCormac, 1991. A chapel side-wall with an accommodation block to the left.

walls, equally likely to be read as non-load-bearing cladding as structure, contrast with the explicitly exposed structure at the Licorne stadium, Amiens, that similarly engenders perceptions of protection and enclosure (see Fig. 3.13).

The exterior structure of the Öhringen Business School represents the antithesis of the symmetry and calmness of the Fitzwilliam College Chapel. Outside the main entrance the exterior structure breaks long established traditions of structural order and rationality (Fig. 4.36). In front of a glazed wall, three cross-braced buttresses appear to be quite haphazardly orientated – their alignment neither relating to the building envelope nor to the interior structure. A similarly unusual relationship exists between the buttresses and the thin steel girts they support. The normal hierarchy of mullions supported by girts that are in turn supported by buttresses is subverted. A girt passes through a buttress without being able to transfer its loads to it (Fig. 4.37).

Exterior structure in this area of the school appears ad hoc and crude. Blundell-Jones notes that this aesthetic is in fact carefully developed and a 'confident use of a vocabulary elaborated over decades'.[9] The architect, Behnisch, is well known for his colliding geometries, layered spaces and careening volumes. Upon entering the atrium, a fragmented and layered structural language contributes to a light and lively, if not exciting, interior space.

▲ **4.36**   Business School, Öhringen, Germany, Guntor Bohnisch & Partner, 1993. The main entrance and the haphazardly orientated buttresses.

▲ **4.37**   A horizontal plate passes through the buttress without making contact.

▲ **4.38**   Olympic Archery Complex, Barcelona, Spain, Miralles and Pinos, 1991. Aimlessly directed columns support slabs passing over the retaining wall.

The 1992 Olympic Archery Complex, Barcelona, also disregards an ordered and rational view of design and building. Where seen from the original archery training fields, the buildings that now function as football changing-rooms exhibit haphazardly orientated roof planes and exposed structural members (Fig. 4.38). Depending on their function, the training field facilities comprise several different architectural forms. For example, spectators shelter under irregularly tilted and cantilevered concrete slabs, while changing-rooms and other facilities are enclosed. The buildings are mostly embedded within the bank they retain.

▲ **4.39** Parc Güell, Barcelona, Spain, Antonio Gaudí, 1914. The retaining structure elegantly expresses resistance to the soil pressure acting upon it.

Their irregular and dynamic architectural and structural forms appear to be expressive, but of what? First, one notes that although the building functions as a retaining wall its structural layout and detailing does not respond to the reality of horizontal soil pressure. Casually inclined columns are no match for slipping soil, stabilized in this case by stone-filled wire cages, and contrast starkly with a nearby construction that also combines retaining and shelter – for at Barcelona's Park Güell, Gaudí exemplifies structure expressing its soil-retaining function clearly and gracefully (Fig. 4.39). Perhaps the forms express aspects of archery? Such a reading seems reasonable. The linearity and random orientation of exposed structure, as well as its dynamic qualities could well refer to arrows in flight or their quivering upon striking a target. However, as one reviewer reports, any expressive qualities primarily express the design process. He writes: 'Let's . . . get straight on to what Miralles likes to remember as being essential to this project. In a nutshell, he reminds us, the project grew out of "rubbing" over other projects and out of the possibilities offered by the need to carry out earth retaining work.'[10] It therefore appears the design process itself is being expressed!

Expressive qualities of the exterior structure at Bracken House, London, an insertion between the end wings of a central demolished block, have clearer and more obvious origins. Structural members are not immediately recognizable from a distance due to their relatively fine scale, made possible by the close proximity of the primary columns, just four metres

▲ **4.40** Bracken House, London, England, Michael Hopkins and Partners, 1991. Main façade.

▲ **4.41** Metal columns, a cantilever bracket and a stainless steel rod behind a stone pier.

behind the façade (Fig. 4.40). The exposed structure includes slender secondary columns, mullion-columns on the exterior bay window corners and ground floor piers supporting the columns (Fig. 4.41).

If an exploration of structural expression begins by considering the slender gun-metal columns, one notes their similarity to the bronze columns of the old building. The scale of both old and new columns and their fineness recalls Gothic attached-shafts. At first floor level where the columns meet their base-brackets, short cantilevers express structural actions. Tapered arms reflect internal bending moments, and a stainless steel rod with its enlarged end connection detail expresses its tensile role in preventing the bracket from over-turning. Solid stone piers carry and express compression, the dominant structural action.

The truss framing the main entrance and supporting the roof canopy also expresses structural actions, and like the columnar structure displays equally high levels of craft and design elegance (see Fig. 7.39). Individually cast and highly refined, its elements exude a sense of quality. Such a high standard of design is consistent with the client's expectation that the building 'shall offer respect to the great architectural achievements of the past, dominate this century and realize the vision of the next'.[11] Quite a demanding brief!

Any discussion on the expressive roles of exterior structure must consider the expression of another important architectural issue – the relationship between a building and its foundations, or in other words, how

▲ **4.42**   Church in Porta, Brissago, Switzerland, Raffaele Cavadini, 1997. Front elevation with a visible gap under the beam.

▲ **4.43**   Splash Leisure Centre, Sheringham, England, Alsop & Lyall, 1988. Wall-to-foundation detailing conveys a lack of grounding.

a building is grounded. At one end of the spectrum an architect might seek to express a strong sense of grounding where a building is read as being rooted to its foundations and growing from them, but other design concepts, as illustrated by the following two examples, express floating or hovering.

At the Porta church, Brissago, ground floor beams that would normally be partially embedded like typical foundation beams are elevated above the ground, creating a 100 mm gap (Fig. 4.42). By visually separating the tiny cube-like church from its foundations the architect conveys a sense of the building 'touching the ground lightly'. This perception of the superstructure being not *of* the site, but rather built *over* it, respects the site's previous occupant; a medieval chapel whose demolition caused considerable controversy.

The lack of any visible structure at the base of the Splash Leisure Centre, Sheringham, conveys the even more extreme impression of the building being transportable (Fig. 4.43). This perception arises from a simple construction detail. The double-layered plywood cladding over-hangs and partially conceals a conventional concrete foundation whose edge sits flush with the inner layer of plywood.

By way of contrast, an effective method to express strong connectivity between a building and its site involves exposing foundations that emerge from the ground and then seamlessly form the superstructure. The Welsh Wildlife Centre, Cardigan, illustrates such an approach using stone blocks (Fig. 4.44). They form a solid plinth that suggests a strong connection between the substructure and the superstructure. Although expressed far less intensely, that same sense of a building being grounded or grafted to

▲ **4.44**   Welsh Wildlife Centre, Cardigan, Wales, Niall Phillips Architects, 1994. Stone plinths visually anchor the building to its site.

its site is observed in two previously discussed buildings, at 88 Wood Street, London (Fig. 4.4), and at the RAC Control Centre, Bristol (Fig. 4.5).

SUMMARY

This chapter illustrates exposed structure enriching the exterior visual qualities of buildings. After over-viewing some of the many contributions exterior structure can make to façades by focusing upon the Hong Kong and Shanghai Bank (Fig. 4.1), the chapter examines the aesthetic impact of exterior structure. Case studies illustrate how structure modulates surfaces and provides a means for introducing often much-desired depth and texture. Structure also screens façades and filters light and views. The importance of suitable structure scale is noted where structure plays any of these roles.

Two sections then explore how structure connects exterior and interior architecture and how it marks and articulates entry into a building. Finally, the chapter provides precedents of structure playing expressive roles. Based on the variety of expression evident in the few examples presented, it would seem that exposed structure is capable, to some degree at least, of expressing any architectural idea or quality.

REFERENCES AND NOTES

1 Williams, S. (1989). *Hong Kong Bank: The Building of Norman Foster's Masterpiece.* Jonathan Cape, p. 85.
2 See, for example, Ogg, A. (1987). *Architecture in Steel: The Australian Context.* Royal Australian Institute of Architects, p. 36.
3 Gale, A. (1995). Not the Western Morning News. *RIBA Journal*, August, p. 39.

4   Quoted in Freeman, A. (1980). The world's most beautiful airport? *AIA Journal*, Nov., p. 47.

5   A gerberette is the cast-steel cantilever beam that acts like a see-saw. It supports an interior truss close to its supporting column, pivots about the column and has its other end tied down to the foundations with a steel tension rod.

6   Quoted in Bussel, A. (2001). Great expectations. *Interior Design*, May, pp. 297–301.

7   For technical information refer to Brown, A. (2000). Stone and tension, in *Peter Rice: The Engineers' Contribution to Contemporary Architecture*. Thomas Telford Ltd, Ch. 12.

8   See the architect's account in Taylor, N. (1990). Pleasure place, the Dome, Doncaster. *The Architects' Journal*, 21 Mar., pp. 39–65.

9   Blundell-Jones, P. (1995). Behnisch in Öhringen. *Architectural Review*, 197 (1178), pp. 32–7.

10 English summary of Lahuerta, J.J. (1992). Il padiglione per il tiro con l'arco. *Abitare*, 307, pp. 208–15.

11 Amery, C. (1992). *Bracken House*. Wordsearch, p. 37.

5

BUILDING FUNCTION

INTRODUCTION

In its exploration of the relationships between structure and building functionality this chapter begins by considering how structure located on the perimeter of a building maximizes spatial planning freedom. A common approach for achieving large structure-free floor areas is to locate primary structure either outside or just inside the building envelope. Next, structure is observed subdividing interior space; first, where the subdivided spaces accommodate similar functions and are perceived as being part of a larger space, and secondly, where structure separates different building functions, like circulation and gallery spaces, from each other. This leads on to a section that examines how structure's physical presence, including its directional qualities, defines and enhances circulation. Finally, examples illustrate structure disrupting function, both deliberately and unintentionally.

Numerous architectural texts acknowledge the need for thoughtful integration of structure with building function. At an essentially pragmatic level, Schodek explains the concept of 'critical functional dimensions.'[1] This approach requires a designer to determine the minimum structure-free plan dimensions for a given space or series of spaces. Once these dimensions are decided upon, 'basic functional modules' can be drawn in plan. Spaces between the modules then determine where vertical structure can be located without intruding upon function. Minimum clear spans across modules can then be readily identified and, together with module shapes, can suggest suitable structural systems such as load-bearing walls or moment-resisting frames in conjunction with one- or two-way floor or roof horizontal spanning systems.

Different-sized modules are often required within one building. For example, the office-sized structural module above ground floor level in the Hôtel du Département, Marseilles, is doubled in size through the use of the X-columns in order to accommodate basement level car parking (see Fig. 3.47). Schodek also discusses briefly the spatial implications of various structural systems, noting the different degrees of directionality they impose upon the spaces they enclose.

Krier takes a broader architectural approach when discussing structure and function. He emphasizes the spatial qualities of different structural systems and insists upon structure and function being integrated: 'Construction is closely related to function. A clearly defined concept of spatial organization demands an appropriate structural solution. The more harmonious this unity, the closer one comes to the architectonic end product.'[2] He categorizes structure which he primarily perceives as a spatial organizer, into three different types: solid wall, skeletal construction, and mixed construction comprising both walls and skeletal structure. Each type possesses a different architectural character. For example, solid walled construction with its introverted and more intimate character contrasts with skeletal structures that are more open and adaptable. Mixed systems, on the other hand, present opportunities for a hierarchy of interior spaces, greater spatial complexity and 'differentiated tectonic character'.

Whereas Krier emphasizes how interior structure, by virtue of its layout and detailing affects spatial character, and therefore function, this chapter concerns itself more directly with the relationship between structure and the physical or practical aspects of building function. The aesthetic impact of structure upon interior space and the inevitability with which it affects function to some lesser extent, is discussed in Chapter 6.

MAXIMIZING FUNCTIONAL FLEXIBILITY

Freedom from structural constraints results in maximum flexibility of space planning and building function. A space clear of interior structure can then be ordered by other architectural elements such as partition walls or screens, if necessary. Clearly, maximum interior architectural flexibility is achieved by positioning primary structure outside the building envelope. Unfortunately, this strategy is often not easily implemented due to possibly excessive structural depths and other architectural implications like cost that are associated with spanning across the whole width of a building. A far more common and realistic approach to achieve a high degree of planning freedom involves adopting the 'free plan' – that integration of structure with interior space inherited from the Modern Movement. Spaces that once would have been enclosed by load-bearing walls now flow almost completely unimpeded around and between columns that are usually located on an orthogonal grid.

A widespread perception exists of the spatial neutrality of structure that enables the 'free plan'. That is, the impact upon interior architecture by structure, perhaps in the form of columns or short walls, whether assessed by its effect upon function or aesthetics, is considered minimal. However, such structure is far from being spatially neutral. Where located within a building envelope it reduces the net usable area as well as restricting space-use in its vicinity. These detrimental effects have been quantified for office buildings. Space loss not only includes the area

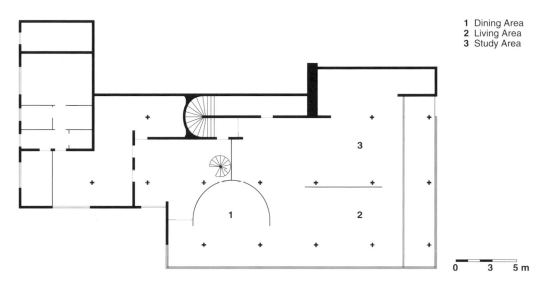

1 Dining Area
2 Living Area
3 Study Area

▲ **5.1** Tugendhat House, Brno, Czech Republic, Mies van der Rohe, 1930. A simplified ground floor plan.

of the structural footprint itself, but also adjacent neutralized areas that are inconvenient for furniture and screen arrangements.[3]

More profound disturbances to building function from so-called 'free plan' structure also arise. Consider, for example, the oft studied Tugendhat House designed by Mies van der Rohe (Fig. 5.1). One reviewer suggests rather uncritically how the architect 'used the columns to help identify places: two of the columns, together with the curved screen wall, frame the dining area; two others help define the living area; and another column suggests the boundary of the study area at the top right on the plan'.[4] However, an alternative reading could view that identification of places as being so unconvincing as to verge on the unintentional. Moreover, after observing the columns positioned close to walls but playing no particular spatially defining architectural roles, and other columns located awkwardly in secondary spaces, one could conclude that the interior architecture would be much improved if the existing walls were to become load-bearing and as many of the non-perimeter columns as possible were removed!

As already mentioned, maximum planning freedom occurs where vertical structure is located on a building's perimeter. This option suits single-storey construction better than multi-storey buildings for two reasons. First, perimeter structure inevitably results in long spans necessitating relatively deep structure and subsequent large inter-storey heights. A deep or high roof structure of a single-storey building does not usually have such severe consequences upon building height as do several layers

▲ **5.2**   Oxford Ice Rink, England, Nicholas Grimshaw & Partners, 1985. Exterior masts and projecting horizontal spine beam.

▲ **5.3**   Financial Times printing works, London, England, Nicholas Grimshaw & Partners, 1988. Exterior columns along the main façade.

of deep floor structure. Secondly, roofs generally weigh far less than suspended floors so they can span greater distances more easily.

Categories of perimeter structure include exoskeletal structures where all structural members lie outside the building envelope, and others, where to differing degrees structure impinges upon interior space. In the second set of buildings, structure either potentially disrupts function around the perimeter of the floor plan, or else it is well integrated with occupancy. Examples of various types of perimeter structure are given below.

According to its architect, a need to reduce building bulk was one of the main reasons for choosing a mast structure for the Oxford Ice Rink, Oxford (Fig. 5.2). Primary structure, in the form of two masts, tension rods and a central spine-beam, carry over 50 per cent of the roof weight. As a consequence of the substantial overall structural depth, equal to the mast height less that of the roof, and the 15 m intervals between supporting tension-rods along its length, the depth of the 72 m long spine-beam is shallow enough to allow the beam to be located under the roofing. Continuous roof beams that span the rink transversely and rest upon the spine-beam at their mid-spans, are supported on slender props located along each eaves line of the main form.

The exterior structure of the Financial Times printing works, London, also facilitates function and allows for flexibility in the future. Perimeter columns line sections of the north and south façades (Fig. 5.3). Their location outside the glass skin they support removes from the approximately 100 m long press-hall any internal structure which could otherwise disturb movement of personnel or paper within the space. Interior structure defining an internal spine-zone parallel to and behind the press

▲ **5.4** Toscana Thermal Pools, Bad Sulza, Germany, Ollertz & Ollertz, 1999. Timber shell structures.

▲ **5.5** Open structure-free space under the shell roofs.

▲ **5.6** Timber Showroom, Hergatz, Germany, Baumschlager-Eberle, 1995. Timber columns project into the showroom.

hall is also walled-off to avoid any structural protrusions into the hall. As well as its functional suitability, this structure-and-skin combination has won over critics by its elegance of detail and sheer transparency. The nightly drama of printing is now highly visible from a nearby road.

By their very nature, shell structures are supported at their perimeters. Although any associated structural elements, such as the ribs that might increase the strength of a shell are usually constructed inside the exterior skin, their structural depths are so shallow as to not reduce space usage significantly. The Toscana Thermal Pools, Bad Sulza, enclosed by glue-laminated timber ribbed-shells, benefit from planning freedom unconstrained by structure (Figs 5.4 and 5.5). Free-flowing interior spaces surround the main pools. As well as providing openness in plan, the shells' ribbed interior surfaces contribute to the attractive interior ambience.

The interior portal frames of the Timber Showroom, Hergatz, are representative of most interior perimeter structures whose vertical members intrude into the building plan (Fig. 5.6). Sometimes, floor plan edge-zones whose widths equal the structural depths can be incorporated unobtrusively into the overall building function. Take Gothic churches, for example, where numerous side chapels slot between deep internal buttresses adjacent to the aisles. At Hergatz, it is of little consequence that structure does not integrate with an edge-zone function. The glue-laminated timber columns are quite shallow, and the exposed frames possess an unusual attractiveness. Here, a conventional engineering system, often relegated to light-industrial buildings, is transformed into one with intrinsic beauty by virtue of its detailing quality. Curves soften the appearance of the frames and invite new architectural interpretations of their

▲ **5.7**   Sainsbury Centre for Visual Arts, Norwich, England, Foster Associates, 1977. The vertical wall structure that is visible on the end elevations houses support functions.

▲ **5.8**   Frankfurt Messenhalle 3, Frankfurt, Germany, Nicholas Grimshaw & Partners, 2001. Buttressing struts and ties for the arched roof structure penetrate the services and circulation zones located along the sides of the hall.

form. Member tapering bestows a lightness and elegance, while unobtrusive connections, such as at the eaves joints, avoid any discordant notes.

At the Sainsbury Centre, Norwich, the perimeter structure lies completely inside the skin (Fig. 5.7). Tubular-steel triangular trusses span between columns of identical cross-section. Although the 2.5 m thick structural walls are unusually bulky, mechanical services, storage and service areas fully occupy all of the space within them. The location and integration of all these secondary functions within the structural depth allows the remainder of the interior to function as a public space free of both vertical structure and 'servant spaces'.

Exhibition Hall 3, Frankfurt, also exemplifies the instance of perimeter structure located within the building envelope well that is integrated with building function (Fig. 5.8). Over the upper exhibition level, tubular-steel arched roof beams span 160 m between triangulated buttresses that are expressed on the end elevations. The buttress depths on each side of the building accommodate the main concourse areas, both horizontal and vertical circulation systems, and service areas. As at the Sainsbury Centre, the entire distance between these perimeter structural zones where measured across the building can be used for exhibition purposes. The first floor structure consists of pairs of storey-deep steel trusses spaced a corridor-width apart in plan, and overlain by beams and a concrete slab. The 32 m spacing between ground floor columns results in a structural grid that also provides a high degree of flexibility for exhibition layouts.

▲ **5.9** Museum of Roman Art, Merida, Spain, Rafael Moneo, 1985. A view along the nave.

▲ **5.10** Floor slabs divide the space vertically.

SUBDIVIDING SPACE

Since antiquity, load-bearing walls have divided building plans into separate spaces. However, since the introduction of metal skeletal-frames in the nineteenth century, non-structural partition walls have provided an expedient alternative. Yet, as observed in contemporary works of architecture, structure still subdivides space. First, several buildings are considered where the interior structural layout within a single large volume creates numerous smaller spaces with similar functions. Further examples then illustrate how interior structure can be configured to create spaces with different functions.

Structure plays significant spatial organizational roles at the Museum of Roman Art, Merida (Figs 5.9 and 5.10). Nine cross-walls subdivide the main space horizontally into separate galleries. A nave, defined by almost full-height arched openings and itself a gallery, forms the main circulation space with smaller galleries off to each side. In the same manner as the brick-clad concrete walls slice through the plan, thin walkways and gallery floors divide the space vertically. A limited structural vocabulary – walls, arches and slabs – transform the potentially empty shell into a series of special architectural spaces that facilitate circulation and the display of artifacts. As well as introducing spatial variety, the combination of structural walls, their rhythm and the hierarchy of different sized arches, greatly enriches if not becomes the interior architecture. Arches range in scale from the prominent nave arches through to those of a more human-scale between the upper galleries, through which only one or two people at a time can pass.

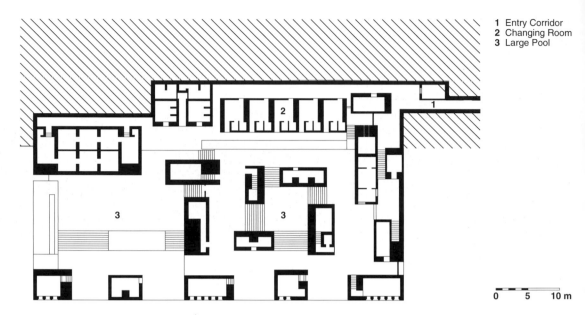

1 Entry Corridor
2 Changing Room
3 Large Pool

0   5   10 m

▲ **5.11** Thermal Baths, Vals, Switzerland, Atelier Peter Zumthor, 1996. Simplified ground floor plan.

Structural walls at the Thermal Baths, Vals, are also the means by which the architect introduces spatial variety. In this building, partially embedded into a hillside slope, narrow light-slots separate turf-covered concrete roof slabs in plan. Vertical support to the roof may be thought of conceptually as a series of large blocks, typically 3 m by 5 m in plan (Fig. 5.11). Constructed from load-bearing composite layered stone with an interior reinforced concrete core, the blocks organize spaces for bathing, circulation and resting. However, as well as defining individual spaces within the main volume of the baths, the blocks themselves are hollowed out. Within each, a bath, unique by virtue of its temperature, lighting or some other quality, or another facility like a massage room, may be discovered. Bathers therefore enjoy extremely varied spatial experiences – from public pools partially enclosed and screened by walls washed by light passing through slots above (Fig. 5.12), to more intimate spaces that are tucked away deep inside the structural blocks.

The Némausus Apartments, Nîmes, is the final example of structure subdividing spaces that accommodate similar functions. Ship-like in form, the apartment building 'floats' on approximately two-hundred relatively slender columns dispersed over a lowered ground floor (Fig. 5.13). Two rudder-shaped shear walls project from its 'stern' to anchor the building longitudinally both physically and conceptually. The structural layout is the major determinant of space usage. At the upper levels, the apartment

▲ **5.12**   Main interior pool, partially surrounded by walls. (Courtesy H. P. Schultz.)

▲ **5.13**   Némausus Apartments, Nîmes, France, Jean Nouvel et Associés, 1988. Columns define car parking and their spacing reflects the widths of the apartments above.

widths are defined by regularly spaced transverse concrete walls which transform into columns at ground level. Car parking occupies this space. Along each side of the building, columns define spaces for pairs of car parks. Although lacking the poetics of the previous two examples, the structure here creates parking bays while maintaining an openness that is conducive to the security of people and vehicles. At first floor and above, structure demarcates individual apartments.

Several buildings now illustrate how structure subdivides space in such a way as to separate quite different functions within it. Like the Thermal Baths, structural ordering of the Contemporary Art Wing, Hamburg, is best appreciated in plan (Figs 5.14 and 5.15). Moving outwards from the central atrium that rises the entire building height, three concentric structural layers are penetrated before entering the galleries. First, two walls define a narrow annulus dedicated to vertical circulation. The next outer zone, also sandwiched between walls, predominately houses service areas. Finally, galleries occupy the majority of space between the third ring of walls around the atrium and the perimeter wall-cum-frame. While structural walls and their space-dividing roles are clear in plan, one of the fascinations of this building is that the walls, even though exposed, are not perceived as structure. All wall surfaces are planar and painted white, evoking a sense of simplicity and purity. Such an emphasis upon surface that leaves visitors without any clues hinting at the materiality or the structural significance of walls, avoids any potential architectural distractions in the vicinity of the exhibited art-works.

▲ **5.19** Education Centre, Newport, Wales, Niall Phillips Architects, 1993. The front of the Centre.

▲ **5.20** A teaching space is separated from the corridor to the right by pairs of columns.

▲ **5.21** Library, Delft Technical University, The Netherlands, Mecanoo Architekten, 1997. A view towards the main entrance.

▲ **5.22** The circulation desk beneath the cone is surrounded by steel struts.

space from an adjacent circulation area behind it (Figs 5.19 and 5.20). The sense of functional separation is accentuated by both the close 2 m spacing between poles, and their pairing which increases the structural density and reflects the repeated paired-poles on the building exterior.

A large cone emerges from the turf roof of the Delft Technical University Library, Delft, which appears to be embedded within a hill (Fig. 5.21). The exposed structure is more than just a virtual projection of the cone surface towards its apex. Near-vertical tension rods support areas of annulus-shaped suspended floors within the cone. The ground floor area beneath the cone is therefore left free of structure. Splayed steel tubes around its circumference surround the circulation desk area, defining it yet distinguishing it from the other library functions within the main hall (Fig. 5.22).

Returning to the Law Courts, Bordeaux, but instead of revisiting the main façade, attention this time focuses upon the public side entrance.

▲ **5.23** Law Courts, Bordeaux, France, Richard Rogers Partnership, 1998. A waiting area under a courtroom pod.

Initially, one is confronted by a timber-clad conical pod outside the glazed skin of the main building, and soon one becomes aware of six others lined up inside. Inclined struts elevate the pods, each housing a courtroom, above concourse level. As well as their structural roles, the struts define informal waiting and meeting areas and separate them from the main circulation route (Fig. 5.23). Eight sloping precast-concrete struts under each pod introduce an informal quality to the spaces. From some vantage points any sense of visual order disappears completely. The struts appear to be assembled chaotically, rejecting any aspirations of a formal interior architecture that alienates some sectors of society. Structure can be read as an informal and perhaps visually confused setting that empathizes with the states-of-mind of those unfortunate enough to visit the courts.

Primary structure at the Kunsthaus, Bregenz, separates vertical circulation from other space usage, in this case, galleries (Fig. 5.24). Best appreciated in plan, the vertical structure consists of only three structural walls, the bare minimum to resist lateral loads in orthogonal directions without the building suffering torsional instability (Fig. 5.25). The asymmetrical layout of the walls presents a challenge for the suspended floors that must span most of the building width. From a view-point located in the middle of any of the four galleries stacked one above the other, structural walls screen off areas of vertical circulation and the grey concrete walls, detailed and constructed with the utmost precision, become the backdrop on which to display art. Visitors remain

▲ **5.27** Colegio Teresiano, Barcelona, Spain, Antonio Gaudí, 1889. The first floor arched corridor.

▲ **5.28** San Cataldo Cemetery, Modena, Italy, Aldo Rossi, 1984. Walls delineating the entrance colonnade recede into the distance.

ground floor plan consists of two spine-walls that create a central corridor with classrooms off either side. At first floor, the load-bearing walls that would be expected above those below are replaced by parabolic arches (Fig. 5.27). The combination of a simple repetitive rhythm arising from their close 1.2 m spacing, their roundedness and whiteness, and the quality of light filtering through from central light-wells conveys a remarkable sense of softness and tranquility.

Although the entrance colonnade to the San Cataldo Cemetery, Modena, is equally as strongly articulated by structure, its aesthetic qualities contrast greatly with those of Colegio Teresiano. Two storeys high and supporting a single storey columbarium above, concrete wall-like arcade columns are very narrow for their height. They create a processional route, extending the entire length of the building (Fig. 5.28). The experience of passing each pair of columns that flank the corridor emphasizes progress along the route which stretches far into the distance. Unless a deliberate turn-of-the-head reveals views between the columns, the perspective along the main axis is framed by what seems like an infinite number of receding walls. While one reviewer refers to the colonnade's 'haunted' quality, it certainly fosters impressions of formality, rawness and joylessness.

The final example where structure defines circulation are the far less sombre, even exuberant, entry canopies to the Bilbao Metro (Fig. 5.29). A transparent skin sheaths eleven tubular-steel arched frames. As well as articulating circulation, other aspects of their design provide a great

▲ **5.29** Bilbao Metro, Bilbao, Spain, Foster and Partners, 1996. Rounded frames express movement to and from an underground station.

deal of architectural enrichment. Note, for example, how the front frame leans slightly outwards over the threshold in a subtle but effective welcoming gesture. While the second frame is orientated vertically, those that follow it lean over incrementally in the other direction until they align normal to the slope of the escalator or stairs inside. Due to their changing orientation from the vertical, the frames invite entry and then graphically indicate in elevation the transition from horizontal to downwards movement. They therefore both express and respond to movements within, and even their roundedness echoes the forms of the underground tunnels and platform areas to which they lead.

Beginning with the Canary Wharf Underground Station, London, several examples illustrate how the *directionality* of exposed structure articulates and enhances circulation. The station's ticket hall, a cathedral-like volume, is visually dominated by a central row of elliptical concrete columns that register its length like marker posts (Fig. 5.30). Although the columns restrict the width of the linear circulation path slightly, their shape and orientation parallel to the flow of commuters minimizes this effect and reinforces the primary axis of movement. A substantial longitudinal spine-beam further accentuates directionality. Its attractively rounded soffit that bears upon sliding-bearings on top of the columns, leads people both into and out of the station via escalators. Ribs cantilever transversely from the spine-beam, hovering like outstretched wings and modulating the vast ceiling. Their relatively small dimensions and transverse orientation do not detract from the linearity imposed on the space by the spine-beam.

Roof structure at the Terminal 3 departure hall, Hamburg Airport, also contributes to circulation by a clear expression of its directionality (Fig. 5.31). Since the roof dimension in the direction of passenger

▲ **5.30** Canary Wharf Underground Station, London, England, Foster and Partners, 1999. The ticket hall with its central columns and spine beam.

▲ **5.31** Terminal 3, Hamburg Airport, Germany, von Gerkan • Marg + Partner, 1991. Roof trusses emphasize the direction of movement on the departures level.

▲ **5.35**   Convent of La Tourette, Eveux, France, Le Courbusier, 1959. The western façade and three levels of irregularly-spaced mullions.

▲ **5.36**   Two columns on the right are set-in from the exterior wall and intrude upon a teaching space.

▲ **5.37**   Pizza Express Restaurant façade, 125 Alban Gate, London, England, Bere Associates, 1996. Deep window mullions limit the café seating layout.

the dual aims of 'floating' the building and freeing-up the façade. Apart from the concrete-walled chapel, the remaining blocks 'touch the ground lightly', and as viewed from the west the complex rhythmical composition of window mullions appear to today's viewers like typical barcode patterns (Fig. 5.35). Unfortunately, while the building exterior is freed from structure, the spatial functionality of the interior suffers considerably. Circular concrete columns severely limit how seating and furniture can be deployed in many of the rooms (Fig. 5.36).

Disruption can also be completely unintended during the design process but evident when a building is completed. Two unrelated examples of disruptive structure are encountered at 125 Alban Gate, London. In the first, deep window mullions intrude upon a first-floor restaurant space. Face-loads on the two-storey-high glazed walls are resisted by mullions in the form of innovatively designed vertical trusses. The truss chords consist of stainless steel rods threaded through glass electrical insulators (Fig. 5.37). The combination of the spacing between these mullions and their depth affects the table layout detrimentally. Unfortunately, the mullion spacing is overly generous for one table, but too close for two, raising the question as to whether the mullions' aesthetic impact justifies the loss of significant usable space.

The second example serves as a reminder of how diagonal members pose a danger to the public. It recalls the full-scale mockups undertaken during the Hong Kong and Shanghai Bank design. During development of a 'chevron' structural scheme, eventually rejected by the client, Foster and Associates placed a polystyrene full-scale diagonal member in their office to assess its danger to passers-by.[9] On the first floor of 125 Alban

▲ **5.38** 125 Alban Gate, London, England, Terry Farrell, 1992. A transfer-truss diagonal member poses a potential danger to passers-by.

▲ **5.39** California College of the Arts, San Francisco, USA, Tanner Leddy Mantum Stacy, 1999. Light steel frames prevent injuries from the 'Nave' brace members.

▲ **5.40** Staatsgalerie, Stuttgart, Germany, Stirling and Wilford, 1984. Columns form a visual barrier around the information desk.

Gate, five one-storey deep transfer-trusses enable the building to span across a road (Fig. 5.38). Truss diagonal tension members, encased in stainless steel tubes, intrude into the public space. To prevent people from injuring their heads, the designers positioned seats and planters to create a safety-zone in the vicinity of the structure.

At the Montgomery Campus, California College of the Arts, San Francisco, the architects provide a more permanent solution to prevent structure-induced injuries. The College occupies a former bus maintenance garage constructed in the 1950s that required seismic retrofitting. Steel chevron frames brace the building in both orthogonal directions. Those orientated transversely define a central interior street (Fig. 5.39). Known as 'The Nave' it has become a successful venue for exhibitions and other events. Light steel frames protrude below waist level from the inclined steel tube braces to prevent any accidents, but just in case these frames are not noticed, rubbish bins are strategically placed alongside.

To conclude this chapter, two buildings illustrate how structure affects building users in unanticipated ways. Within an entry foyer at the Staatsgalerie, Stuttgart, a circular colonnade rings an information desk (Fig. 5.40). Due to the large column sizes and their close spacing they visually form a cylindrical wall that reads more like an attempt to restrict access than to encourage it, and this reduces accessibility to the desk.

A final rather quirky example reiterates the potential danger to people from diagonal structure positioned below head-height. At the Scottish Exhibition Centre, Glasgow, the main concourse passes under a series of pitched portal frames supporting a glazed skin. The portals are

▲ **5.41**   Scottish Exhibition Centre, Glasgow, Scotland, Parr Partnership, 1985. Knee pads on truss-columns.

triangular-sectioned tubular steel trusses with clearly expressed pin bases (Fig. 5.41). An elegant convergence of the three chord members onto a chamfered cylindrical base can not redeem the unfortunate situation where people sitting in a café area strike their heads against the structure. A more elegant solution than the protective-pads might have been the creative deployment of planters, as observed elsewhere in the building.

SUMMARY

In order to explore how structure contributes to and enhances building functionality this chapter begins by reviewing two design strategies to achieve building functionality – one based on identifying and applying 'critical functional dimensions', and a second more general architectural approach. The question of how to maximize functional flexibility is addressed with reference to the 'free plan'. Examples then illustrate how perimeter structures with diverse spatial relationships to their building envelopes allow the most flexible planning and usage of interior spaces.

Two groups of buildings illustrate how structure also contributes to building function by subdividing space. In the first group, the spatial sub-division of a large volume enables similar functions to occur in each small space. Several of the buildings are notable for the diversity of spatial experience and architectural qualities they provide. In the second group, interior subdivision leads to a different space-use in each of the subdivided areas. Typical examples include the structure separating circulation from other spaces such as waiting areas and galleries.

Circulation is a necessary function of any building and is frequently defined or articulated by structural elements such as arcades and frames. Depending on numerous factors including structural spacing, scale, materiality and detailing, structurally defined routes can be read and experienced very differently. For example, while one corridor exudes tranquility, another conveys impressions of rawness and joylessness. Even if the physical presence of structure is insufficiently strong to define circulation, it can enhance it by conveying a sense of directionality.

The concluding section considers works of architecture where structure disrupts function. In most of these cases where structure frustrates building users, architects have given greater priority to the realization of other architectural objectives. Examples illustrate that causes of disruptive structure range from completely intentional to purely accidental reasons.

This chapter illustrates the profound influence structure can have upon building function. By virtue of its permanence, structure both defines and limits the activities within a building. The degree of subtlety with which this is achieved depends upon the extent of the structure's physical presence both in plan and section. Whether it is maximizing functional flexibility or disrupting it, subdividing space or articulating function, structure must be thoroughly integrated both with the design concept and the functional requirements of the building.

REFERENCES AND NOTES

1 Schodek, D. L. (2001). *Structures*, 4th edn. Prentice Hall, p. 468.
2 Krier, R. (1988). *Architectural Composition*. Academy Editions, Rizzoli, p. 27.
3 Davis, G., Thatcher, C. and Blair, L. (1993). *Serviceability Tools Volume 1: Methods for Setting Occupant Requirements and Rating Buildings*. The International Centre for Facilities, Ottawa.
4 Unwin, S. (1997). *Analysing Architecture*. Routledge, p. 137.
5 Quoted in an extensive analysis of architectural form in Ching, F. D. D. (1996). *Architecture: Form, Space & Order*, 2nd edn. Van Nostrand Reinhold, p. 14.
6 Cook, P. (1996). *Primer*. Academy Editions, p. 84.
7 Hale, J. A. (2000). *Building Ideas*. John Wiley & Sons, pp. 87–8.
8 Steel, C. (1996). Tame at heart. *Blueprint*, 127, pp. 3–6.
9 Williams, S. (1989). *Hong Kong Bank: The Building of Norman Foster's Masterpiece*. Jonathan Cape, p. 105.

6 INTERIOR STRUCTURE

INTRODUCTION

Inevitably, some overlap occurs between the previous chapter, which explored the relationships between interior structure and building function, and this chapter. Chapter 5 examined how structure subdivides space in order to physically separate different functions and accommodate them in their own spaces, and how it defines and identifies other important functions, such as circulation. This chapter, however, is not concerned about how structure affects building function in a practical or physical sense – rather, it considers how structure contributes to the architectural qualities and characters of interior spaces.

Many architects believe that there is far more to the relationship between structure and building function than merely meeting physical spatial requirements. If the design approach of Peter Cook is typical, these practical needs are almost taken as given, in order that the real architectural challenge can begin.[1] Cook develops the structural strategy of a building by first designing the 'primary elements'. This means adopting a certain structural concept such as the use of a structural spine, be it a wall or a corridor of columns. As the issue of integrating structure with function is not raised explicitly, it can be assumed the need for fully functional spaces has been attended to during the development of the structural concept. He then turns his attention to 'secondary elements', by which he means individual structural members like beams and columns. Before deciding how to design them, he asks a series of questions: 'Is it a highly rhetorical building with a rhetorical structure? Is the structure to be the muted element? Is the aim for lightness or for a certain emphasis of presence that may contrast with another part of the building? Is the roof to be 'read' as one or do we want the interval of the elements to be staccato, busy, cosy or symbolic of technicality?'[2]

These questions that suggest but a few of the possibilities that this chapter explores, acknowledge the potential for exposed structure to enrich interior architecture visually and conceptually. The extent to which this occurs depends on a variety of factors. Where structural members contrast with adjacent surfaces or architectural elements by means of colour, materiality, depth or texture, structural exposure is heightened. For example, naturally finished timber members stand out against a light-coloured background. Sometimes exposed structural elements may not even be perceived as structure if they are unusually shaped, or if they are visually undifferentiated from other non-structural elements, like partition walls. The effectiveness of any degree of structural exposure must be evaluated in terms of how the exposure, or lack of it, contributes architecturally. Visual exposure of structure, if at all, must enhance the design concept and result in compelling and coherent architecture. After all, although bland and monotonous interior environments are required in some instances, such as to achieve a necessary standard of hygiene, they are not generally conducive to human habitation, and are usually an anathema to architects.

As for the content of this chapter, the next section illustrates how structure enlivens interior surfaces. Structure makes similar contributions inside buildings as it does to exterior building surfaces (Chapter 3), such as modulating, patterning and providing texture. The chapter then continues with examples of interior space enhancement by spatial rather than surface deployment of structure. In some buildings, structure encourages habitation by its density and small-scaled members. In others, large sized structural members might tend to overwhelm occupants. It is noted how structure orders plans, creates spatial hierarchy, introduces visual diversity and injects a sense of dynamism into a space. Finally, the expressive potential of interior structure is examined. Examples include structure expressing a wide diversity of ideas and responding to such issues as site, building function and geometry.

SURFACE STRUCTURE

This section illustrates how interior exposed structure contributes architecturally by modulating and texturing surfaces. Any interior structure that is connected to, or positioned immediately adjacent to the building skin, is considered surface structure.

In contrast to most exterior structural elements, the interior exposed structure considered in this book, particularly in low-rise construction, is more likely to consist of timber than any other structural material. Without having to contend with potentially destructive sunlight and moisture, timber members and their connections are well suited to interior conditions. Consider one of the four roof structures Calatrava designed as set-pieces for the Wohlen High School. The roof covers a squat drum at the centre of the school entrance foyer (Fig. 6.1). The structure is conceptually simple. Sloping rafters radiate from a supporting concrete ring beam to prop a central lantern. However, articulation

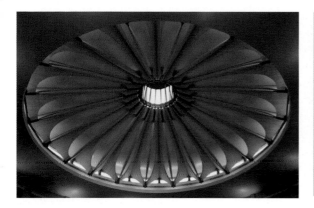

▲ **6.1**   Entrance foyer roof, Wohlen High School, Switzerland, Santiago Calatrava, 1988. Attractive structural roof framing pattern.

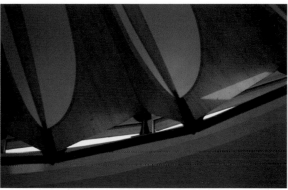

▲ **6.2**   Refined timber struts connect to the steel rod tension-ring and the rafters with deepened ends.

▲ **6.3**   Saint Benedict Chapel, Sumvtg, Switzerland, Peter Zumthor, 1989. Chapel exterior.

of different structural actions introduces a constructional and visual complexity that modulates the interior roof surface and forms a most attractive pattern.

Calatrava has separated two of the structural functions performed by the rafters – that of propping the lantern and the central area of the roof, and secondly, transferring the roof weight to each end of the rafters by bending and shear. Timber spindle-shaped struts perform the propping duties. They fit into conical steel shoes, which at the lower ends of the rafters connect to two elements, the ends of the V-shaped rafters themselves and a circumferential tension-ring consisting of three steel rods (Fig. 6.2). The tension-ring absorbs the horizontal component of strut thrusts while the vertical component is transferred upwards through the deep end-sections of the glue-laminated rafters. They load short steel stub-columns that bear on the surrounding ring beam and provide enough height for a short circular clerestory drum. The entry of natural light, restricted to the glazed lantern and the clerestory, accentuates the radiating pattern of the structure. The petal-shaped roof soffit surfaces and the structure below them are reminiscent of a flower head.

Saint Benedict Chapel, Sumvtg, offers another very attractive example of interior surface modulation. In this case, structure graces both the roof and the walls. Situated on the steep slope of an alpine valley, the chapel is tear-drop or leaf-shaped in plan. Outside, curved timber shingle-clad walls rise to a horizontal glazed and vertically louvred band below the shallow roof. Given the absence of visible support to the roof, it appears disconnected from the enclosing wall below and 'hovers' (Fig. 6.3).

▲ **6.4** Chapel interior, facing towards the altar.

▲ **6.5** Ribbed roof structure.

Inside the chapel, the roof support is revealed. Thirty-six regularly spaced square posts are set out from the interior plywood wall-lining (Fig. 6.4). Each connects delicately to the wall by three steel pins. The simple move of withdrawing the posts from their conventional location within the walls and exposing them affects the interior enormously. Acting as visual markers, they modulate the wall surface, but also increase the shape definition of the interior space and accentuate a sense of enclosure by their continuous alignment with the roof ribs they support.

The roof structure possesses symmetry and visual simplicity. The ribbed pattern of rafters recalls the ribs on the underside of a leaf (Fig. 6.5). Whereas conventional roof framing usually comprises a hierarchical structure consisting of transverse rafters above a deeper longitudinal spine or ridge-beam, all the chapel roof ribs, including the spine-beam that does not span the whole length of the chapel, are of identical depth, and each branches from the spine to bear on a perimeter post. Thin steel plates, welded together to achieve the branching geometry, are interleaved between timber laminates to achieve a two-way structural action. Skilfully concealed, the reinforcement does not detract from the glue-laminated timber construction. Further evidence of detailing refinement is seen in the shape of the spine-beam itself. Not only trapezoidal in cross-section to soften its visual impact, its width tapers in harmony with the building plan, wide near the front of the chapel and narrow at the rear. These details that reflect the building form and the designer's aesthetic sensibility are indiscernible at the first viewing, but

▲ **6.6**   FDA Laboratory, Irvine, California, USA, Zimmer Gunsul Frasca Partnership + HDR, 2003. The perimeter wall of the library with its internal buttresses.

contribute significantly to the simple beauty of the exquisite interior structure.

At the FDA Laboratory, Irvine, California, surface modulation is taken to another degree of intensity in the library. Not only does structure modulate the interior wall areas, but due to its considerable depth it also plays a spatial subdivisional role around the perimeter of the space. The library is semi-circular in plan, essentially enclosed within reinforced concrete walls. Supporting the ends of beams that radiate from the centre of the semi-circle, deep cast-in-place buttresses project into the room (Fig. 6.6). They subdivide the wall circumference into six equal segments, each of which has its own sense of partial enclosure. A desk placed in each segment benefits from natural light through a central slit window and a perimeter skylight above whose width matches the increased depth of the buttresses at roof level.

Ceiling structure, together with inclined columns, considerably enriches the interior space of the Güell Colony Crypt, Barcelona. Rough hewn stone columns, precisely angled in accordance with Gaudí's catenary analytical study, form an inner semi-circular arcade around the sanctuary.[3] This centralized structure focuses attention on the sanctuary and the particularly richly textured ceiling above it (Fig. 6.7). Shallow and audaciously thin brick arches support a brick soffit. The construction method, more common in timber than brick, has secondary members bearing on top of, rather than in the same plane as, the primary members.

▲ 6.7   Güell Colony Crypt, Barcelona, Spain, Antonio Gaudí, 1917. Columns support an inner arcade ring and the textured ceiling above.

Secondary ribs generally radiate toward the perimeter of the crypt from two circular nodes in front of the altar.

Westminster Lodge, Dorset, is one of several experimental timber buildings at Hooke Park that explores environmental architecture. It consists of eight single-bedrooms gathered around a central 8 m by 8 m living space. Roundwood thinnings, not normally considered of structural value, comprise its structure. Extensive research and development of pole-splices and other connection details confirmed the structural adequacy of this form of pole construction. After poles were spliced, they were bent to form a grillage of interlocking beams that span the main space and form the shallow curved roof (Fig. 6.8). The beams consist of two pole-chords spaced apart by timber blocks. Diagonal timber sarking that bears on the upper level of the poles, carries the weight of a turf roof.

Although exposed poles and lintels modulate the interior painted plasterboard walls and further express the roundwood framing system, the roof structure has a greater aesthetic presence in the interior space. The following factors combine to achieve a most visually satisfying roof structure – the close 600 mm grillage module, the gentle roof curvature that reflects the relative ease of bending small-diameter green poles, the depth and stratification of the five horizontal layers of structural members including the sarking, a level of structural complexity that can be comprehended, and finally, a natural peeled and trimmed pole finish.

▲ **6.8** Westminster Lodge, Hooke Park, Dorset, England, Edward Cullinan Architects, 1996. A grillage of roundwood beams spans the main space.

▲ **6.9** Building Industry School, Hamm, Germany, Heger Heger Schlieff, 1996. Lamella timber vaults span the workshop.

Exposed timber structure also enriches the interior surfaces of the next two buildings. As at Westminster Lodge, where structural form and materiality reflect a commitment to ecological sustainability, the timber roofs of the Building Industry School, Hamm, also possess a similar pedagogical value (Fig. 6.9). Seven timber lamella vaults that span between glue-laminated beams, roof the workshops. Four of the repeated vaults cover an interior hall-like volume while the other three shelter outdoor activities. Structure contributes a distinctive and attractive ceiling pattern to all the spaces.

Saint Massimiliano Kolbe church, Varese, exemplifies another building with aesthetically pleasing interior timber structure. Not only is the white hemispherical form in a northern Italian suburban setting unexpected, but so is its interior consisting of timber lining over a triangulated glue-laminated timber dome (Fig. 6.10). The primary triangulating ribs, the horizontal members between them and the lining are all stained white. The structural members, with their curved profiles, are sympathetic to the enclosing spherical geometry of the main congregational space and modulate its interior surface. Relative to the size of the enclosed volume, the small member sizes are a reminder of the structural efficiency of a braced dome.

Most of the connections between the timber members are concealed, but the architect has chosen to celebrate the joints between primary members (Fig. 6.11). The detail possesses similar qualities to Fay Jones' much admired Thorncrown Chapel connections where light passes through the timber joints.[4] Although the exterior cladding prohibits any

▲ **6.10**   Saint Massimiliano Kolbe church, Varese, Italy, Justus Dahinden, 1994. Interior surface.

▲ **6.11**   A typical joint between ribs.

transparency in the Varese church, the structural connections decorate the interior surface like a setting of widely spaced jewels. The architect has certainly achieved his aim of avoiding 'awe-inspiring and intimidating spaces . . . that make a totalitarian impression' and designed a space that is 'sheltering, protective and should inspire trust'.[5]

▲ **6.12** Sondica Airport Terminal, Bilbao, Spain, Santiago Calatrava, 2000. Ribs cantilever under the departure level forecourt.

For the final example of structure enlivening interior surfaces the new terminal at Sondica Airport, Bilbao, is visited. Huge cantilever ribs dominate the ground floor entry area while supporting the departure level forecourt and roading above (Fig. 6.12). From a maximum depth of approximately 3 m, the ribs taper towards their tips and merge with the concrete slab they support. They prepare visitors to the terminal for an architectural language of ribs within its interior.

In the main concourse, curved steel ribs radiate from the top of an inclined column to encompass the triangular plan of the whole space (Fig. 6.13). Part-way along their lengths the ribs are supported by a shallow steel arch, triangular in cross-section, which enhances the sweeping ribbed aesthetic. Structural ribs not only pattern the ceiling but also form all the window mullions, continuing the ribbed theme that dominates both the interior and exterior architecture of the terminal.

Although all the previous buildings exemplify attractive exposed structure it is worth cautioning the reader that surface structure, and in fact any exposed structure for that matter, may invite readings that are unintended by its designers. For example, a reviewer of the Great Court roof at the British Museum, London (see Fig. 3.55), observes:

From the ground, one is very aware of the geometric juxtapositions the roof makes with the existing forms in stone, particularly around the porticoes. Grids like this are by their nature non-hierarchical, but it is a Modernist fantasy that this means they are neutral. What the roof does is reinforce the

▲ **6.13** Ribs radiate over the entire terminal ceiling.

impression that the Great Court is not a place to linger, but a space to move through; the swirling vortex of its geometry, which Buro Happold wrote its own software to resolve, is curiously restless from many angles of view.[6]

Although the architects did not intend to convey such a sense of restlessness, they would no doubt view this reading as a price to be paid for a scheme that roofs the courtyard in a most elegant manner.

SPATIAL STRUCTURE

An underlying premise of this chapter is that spatial structure, such as a free-standing column, has a tangible impact upon the space around it. Ching explains this effect: 'when located within a defined volume of space, a column will generate a spatial field about itself and interact with the spatial enclosure', and 'when centered in a space, a column will assert itself as the center of the field and define equivalent zones of space between itself and the surrounding wall planes'.[7] But this is not to say that spatial structure contributes positively to the making of architectural space.

Consider, for example, free-plan column grids. Although they enhance constructability, they do not have the same effect on interior architecture. Such regular structural layouts are unlikely to be read positively. Van Miess expresses his concern: 'Some spaces have great difficulty becoming places. Let us take the example of the "neutral" spaces of large open-plan offices . . .' He continues by explaining how the Centraal Beheer office structure at Apeldoorn, *does* respond to the need for place-making (see Fig. 5.26).[8] Erickson, also critical of the free plan, writes: 'The open space grids of Mies and Corbu, for instance, are in retrospect both architectural and structural copouts as they do not respond directly to the particular spatial environments and have little to do with the genius of their architecture.'[9]

In spite of the architectural limitations of regular and rectilinear column grids, we must acknowledge the significant roles such structure does play in ordering space. Somewhat ironically, Centre Pompidou, Paris (see Fig. 4.18), a building with extensive floor-plate areas that offer almost unlimited planning flexibility, is criticized for its lack of ordering structure. A reviewer bemoans: 'It is even tempting to wonder if columns might have been an asset, or the interruption of circulation or fixed service cores – anything to impose some architectural discipline in the vast interior. . . . Yet it does seem that Piano & Rogers have played all their good cards on the highly expressive exterior of the building, leaving themselves not much with which to win our admiration inside.'[10] In

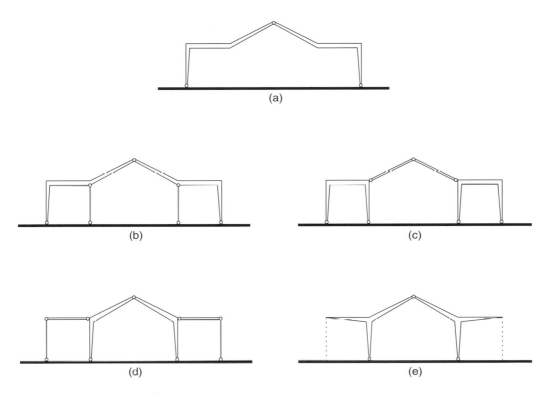

▲ 6.14   Different structural layouts affect how spaces are read. (After Ogg)

many buildings though, particularly those providing open-plan office accommodation, while column grids may be read optimistically as ordering space, they are more likely to be spatially disruptive.

The influence of spatial structure upon interior spaces of a building can be further appreciated by considering Fig. 6.14.[11] Within an identical building envelope very different spatial qualities arise by varying interior structural layouts, all of which are feasible from a structural engineering perspective. While the whole internal volume is essentially perceived as one space in options (a) and (b), (c) and (d) each provide two separate and differentiated spatial zones. Option (e) offers the opportunity of creating a closer relationship between the inside and outside.

A similar investigation of alternative structural layouts and their influence upon interior space can be, and should be performed on any building at the preliminary design stage. Figure 6.15 presents different lateral-load resisting layouts for a regular four-storey building. Variations to moment-resisting frames that resist transverse wind and earthquake

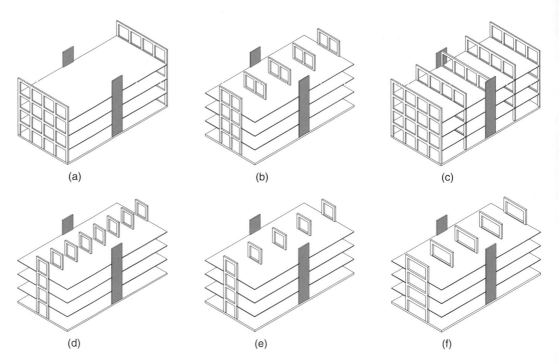

▲ **6.15**   Alternative structural layouts for resisting transverse lateral loads on a multi-storey building.

loads only are shown. In each case the same two shear walls provide longitudinal stability. Gravity-only columns are not shown. As in the previous figure, each structural option contributes a unique spatial character to every floor that can strengthen the design intent. The six options are but just a taste of the huge range of possibilities. For example, the next stage of the exploration might involve shifting some or all of the one and two-bay frames off the building centreline – perhaps placing them on a curved line running between the ends of the building. While the structural performance is unaltered, such a move could create a particularly innovative and memorable building interior.

The following buildings illustrate the diverse range of architectural qualities that interior structure can help achieve. To begin, several spaces where structure itself creates a strong impression of being inhabited are examined. That is, occupants sense they inhabit structure that is located within a larger volume, rather than inhabiting the overall volume itself.

First, design studios in two schools of architecture are considered. In both, high spatial structural density and small-scale structural members

▲ **6.16** Portland Building, University of Portsmouth, England, Hampshire County Council Architects Department, 1996. The timber framework creates spatial zones within a studio.

▲ **6.17** Lyons School of Architecture, Lyons, France, Jourda et Perraudin, 1988. Structure breaks up a large studio area.

create human-scale spaces. At the Portland Building, Portsmouth, an orthogonal post-and-beam framework supports the roof and creates a series of subdivided zones (Fig. 6.16). Spatial zoning is emphasized by how the architects have treated the framework as an insertion into the space and visually quite distinct from the roof. Although the roof slopes, the beams of the interior framework remain horizontal and thereby strengthen their definition of the smaller sub-spaces.

The double-height first-floor studios at the Lyons School of Architecture are broken up far more emphatically by the diagonal glue-laminated timber struts that prop the roof (Fig. 6.17). Mezzanine work spaces hang from the roof structure and create even more intimate working areas and spatial diversity within the large volumes. Students are never more than a metre or two away from a structural element, be it a strut or a mezzanine floor tension-tie. Although such a dense spatial structure limits how the studio space can be used, it creates a strong sense of fostering habitation and of framing activities occurring within the studios.

That same sense of the immediacy of structure is present in the Wohlen High School hall. In plan, regular column spacing articulates a central nave and side aisles. However, in section and when observed three-dimensionally, structure takes a far less conventional form. Free-standing roof support structure within the enclosing concrete walls dominates the interior (Figs 6.18 and 6.19). Gracefully curved pedestals support timber arches, and the radiating ribs create a delicate and intricate rhythmical structure. The frequency of ribs, their spatial orientation with respect to each other and the arches, and their white stain finish

▲ **6.18**   Hall, Wohlen High School, Switzerland, Santiago Calatrava, 1988. A view towards the rear of the hall.

▲ **6.19**   Looking across the hall.

make this structure so appealing. While timber details lack any elaboration, the precast concrete pedestals exhibit strong sculptural qualities. From a functional viewpoint the interior structure limits the hall's flexibility, but on the positive side it creates a wonderful and unique interior space.

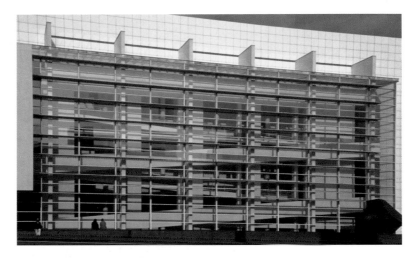

▲ **6.20**   Museum of Contemporary Art, Barcelona, Spain, Richard Meier Architects, 1995. Exterior glazed wall to the ramp-hall with the ramp structure behind.

▲ **6.21**   Ramp colonnade to the right and the innermost structural layer on the left.

Building users also intimately experience interior structure within the full-height atrium of the Museum of Contemporary Art, Barcelona. Continuing the theme of layering that is evident on the main façade, the atrium or ramp-hall contains three layers of vertical structure (Figs 6.20 and 6.21). Just inside the skin, a layer of thin rectangular columns support the roof and the three-storey glazed wall. Next, a free-standing colonnade interspersed with several non-structural vertical elements that also read as structure, carries ramps which cantilever from both sides of the columns. Beyond the ramp structure in a direction away from the glazed wall, the third layer of structure takes the form of another colonnade in front of the balconies and supporting beams emanating from the main galleries. The ramp-hall width is therefore defined by colonnades and inhabited by another carrying the ramps. Structure therefore plays a powerful role in spatial modulation. When ascending or descending the ramps, gallery visitors move past and close to these layers of vertical structure. Proximity to the structure and a rhythmical engagement with it all contribute to a sense of inhabiting it.

Consideration of structure engendering a sense of being inhabited now leads to examples where structure plays more dynamic and dramatic roles, beginning with the Philharmonie auditorium, Berlin. The fragmentation of its surfaces used so effectively to break up undesirable sound reflections in the main auditorium, continues into the main foyer. Two pairs of raking columns support the underside of the sloping auditorium

▲ **6.22**   Philharmonie, Berlin, Germany, Hans Scharoun, 1963. Some of the diverse structural elements in the foyer.

▲ **6.23**   Stadttor Building, Dusseldorf, Germany, Petzinka Pink und Partner, 1998. An interior braced tower is visible through the glazing.

floor (Fig. 6.22). The foyer space is visually dynamic with many different structural elements – columns, piers, walls and bridges that support floors, circulation elements like staircases and walkways, and horizontal and sloping ceilings. The structure appears irregular, even spontaneous, and certainly not constrained to an orthogonal grid. The spatial profusion, density and diversity of the structural and circulation elements possess striking spatial qualities similar to those in Piranesi's *Carcere* etchings.

The Stadttor Building, Dusseldorf, provides another example of dramatic interior structure (Fig. 6.23). Two huge tubular-steel towers, located near diagonally opposing corners in plan, resist lateral loads. The architect has separated the gravity and lateral load resisting systems and chosen to express the latter. The concrete-filled structural steel members are massive by comparison to the light gravity-only columns whose small dimensions increase the building's transparency elsewhere in plan.

The braced towers are awe-inspiring in scale. The fact that they occupy voids and are themselves open, their height uninterrupted by floor slabs, means their entire size can be observed from many interior (and exterior) vantage points. Like giant masts, the structural towers are a defining characteristic of a building already endowed with other special features such as a vast atrium and extensive glazed façades. In terms of

▲ **6.25** Fitzwilliam College Chapel, Cambridge, England, Richard MacCormac, 1991. Concrete frames demarcate a central area.

▲ **6.24** A view up through a tower.

impact upon interior space, the towers with their diagonal braces are visually dynamic, but at the same time their scale is rather overwhelming. Patrons of a ground floor café situated near the base of a mast look up through the mast to the ceiling some 58 m above (Fig. 6.24). One can not imagine a less intimate and cosy interior space.

The next two examples of spatial structure lack any sense of the structural drama observed in the two previous examples, but illustrate how structure in a state-of-repose plays important spatial ordering roles.

Having discussed previously the rounded and protective exterior wall structure of Fitzwilliam College Chapel, Cambridge (see Fig. 4.35), the impact of a completely different structural system upon its interior space is examined. Three independent concrete frame structures stand within the confines of the chapel's walls. The central structure of four columns forms two frames in both orthogonal directions (Fig. 6.25). Together with the lowered concrete ceiling slab, the frames demarcate an area square in plan, centred between the walls. Two identical one-way frames flank the sides of this central structure. They are separated far enough from it to be read as independent frames, and with a large enough gap to house hot-water radiators. The four frames that align parallel to the major axis of the chapel therefore read as two sets of layered structure. The outer frames carry most of the weight of the timber roof that bears on inclined timber struts and cantilevers from them towards the curved walls (Fig. 6.26).

▲ **6.26** The timber roof is propped off an outer frame.

▲ **6.27** Nôtre Dame du Raincy, Paris, France, Auguste Perret, 1923. Church interior with its four rows of columns.

The interior frames set up a spatial hierarchy. Essentially they denote the importance of the liturgical activities by 'enclosing' the space occupied by the altar and sanctuary. The choice of white polished precast concrete for the frames further reinforces the importance of this space. Stairs and side seating occupy left-over spaces to each side of the frames. The space to the rear of the central frames accommodates most of the congregation, the organ and an additional staircase.

The second example, La Nôtre Dame du Raincy, Paris, also exemplifies structure ordering space (Fig. 6.27). Considered by some to be the world's first masterpiece of reinforced concrete architecture, its plan is typical of the neo-Gothic churches of that era. The church is five full bays long with an additional half-bay at each end. Four columns divide the width into two aisles and a central nave. The roof structure reinforces this tripartite order. A vaulted ceiling that relies on hidden transverse upstand-ribs for its support, runs the length of the nave while short aisle vaults are orientated transversely. Structural layout in plan appears to be based on a previous church design for the site, except that those original bay lengths were doubled by the architect to approximately 10 m.[12]

This modification immediately opened up the whole interior, reducing the distinction between nave and aisles and resulting in a lighter and more subtle ordering of space. Columns modulate both the whole volume as well as the side walls. Placing columns just inside the skin

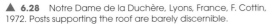

▲ **6.28** Notre Dame de la Duchère, Lyons, France, F. Cottin, 1972. Posts supporting the roof are barely discernible.

▲ **6.29** The exterior wall is structurally separated from the roof by glazing.

rather than incorporating them into the wall maintains a clear distinction between the structure and the visually arresting pre-cast concrete and coloured glass building envelope. This relationship between columns and skin is also considered to increase the sense of spaciousness within the church.[13] The columns do not compete with the skin for attention but rather their slenderness and wide spacing enable them to blend in with it.

Before completing this discussion on how structure contributes to the spatial qualities of interior space a final example demonstrates an architectural concept that requires vertical structure to become almost invisible.

In the church of La Nôtre Dame de la Duchère, Lyons, its vertical structure fades into the background. Four slender cantilevered steel posts support the whole roof and also resist all the lateral loads acting on the building above eaves level. Lateral loads on the perimeter walls are resisted by regularly spaced columns incorporated into self-supporting walls that also cantilever from their foundations. Compared to the scale of the deep glue-laminated timber roof beams and the visual solidity of the ceiling, the posts are barely discernible (Fig. 6.28). Continuous strip windows that separate the perimeter columns and walls from the roof, reinforce the impression of the roof hovering (Fig. 6.29).

EXPRESSIVE STRUCTURE

The last section of this chapter focuses upon structure playing expressive roles. Examples of both surface and spatial interior structure instance structure expressing a wide range of ideas. The structures of

▲ **6.30**   Museum of Gallo-Roman Civilization, Lyons France, Bernard Zehrfuss, 1975. A central row of continuous and sloping columns.

▲ **6.31**   Concrete frames extend over the galleries and corridor. The sloping columns express the hill-side embedment of the building.

the first two buildings express resistance to external horizontal loads, while those that follow express aspects related to building usage and geometry.

Five floors of the Museum of Gallo-Roman Civilization, Lyons, are embedded in a hillside adjacent to an ancient amphitheatre. Apart from an uppermost entrance and reception level, the only other visible evidence of the museum are two small viewing galleries that project from the sloping face of the hill to overlook the nearby ruins, and vehicular access doors at the lowest level. Reinforced concrete frames rise up through the building and support suspended floor slabs (Fig. 6.30).

A strong structural presence permeates the underground volume. Large beams and columns project into galleries and modulate the spaces. Fortunately, their sensitive detailing avoids any undue structural severity. Curved junctions between beams and columns, and ceilings and walls, and tapered cross-sections of the beams soften the otherwise visual hardness of the concrete structure. Resistance to the lateral soil pressures acting on the rear wall is to some extent expressed by the general heaviness of the frame members, but is achieved primarily by the inclination of the outermost and central columns (Fig. 6.31). Their slope, which also reflects that of the vegetated hillside outside, expresses the structural buttressing often necessary to resist soil pressures.

The exposed structure at Westminster Station on the London Underground Jubilee Line also expresses the presence of external earth pressures. In the access-tunnels and around the train platforms, curved metal

▲ **6.32**   Westminster Station, London, England, Michael Hopkins & Partners, 1999. Tunnel lining exposed at a platform.

▲ **6.33**   Horizontal props between side walls.

tunnel liners, plates and bolts speak the unique language of underground construction (Fig. 6.32). However, the structure expresses the external pressures most clearly in the main hall (Fig. 6.33). Designed to be as open as possible, this huge 35 m high hall houses seventeen escalators and numerous floors that service the various lines that pass through

▲ **6.35**   Kunsthal, Rotterdam, The Netherlands, Office for Metropolitan Architecture, 1992. Columns in the auditorium lean towards the dais.

▲ **6.34**   Props pass through a central column.

the station. To add to its spatial complexity, eighteen 660 mm diameter horizontal steel struts pass across the hall and through a central row of vertical columns interspersed by cross-bracing. Welcome to another Piranesian space!

Both the surface and the spatial structure express the presence of external soil pressure. The hall side-walls are deeply patterned by a vertical grillage of projecting piers and horizontal beams. Interior surfaces that are recessed within these members present a rough shotcrete-like finish, often associated with soil retention. This quite massive surface wall structure, insufficient in itself to protect the hall walls from inwards collapse, is propped apart by circular solid cast-steel struts. The manner in which they are recessed into the wall structure at their ends expresses their role as compression struts. They read as thrusting into the wall and locally deforming it. At the centrally placed columns, projecting collars to the struts express the horizontal continuity required of the compression struts (Fig. 6.34).

Structure expresses different aspects of building use in the next four buildings. At the Kunsthal, Rotterdam, structure expresses a number of ideas. First, and at the most basic level, columns supporting the auditorium roof slope forward towards the dais (Fig. 6.35). By remaining orthogonal to the inclined plane of the auditorium floor the sloping columns focus attention to the front of the space – mimicking how people lean forward, eager to hear and see.

▲ **6.36**   Unusually configured roof-plane bracing.

In other areas of the building, structure expresses qualities of the unexpected nature of the art on display. Within the Hall 2 gallery roof-plane, what appear to be irregular red-coloured bracing elements flash overhead as they pass between translucent truss cladding (Fig. 6.36). To the viewer these members form an unrecognizable pattern, raising the question as to whether or not they are structural.

Balmond, the structural engineer, explains:

> *In Hall 2 of Kunsthal a thin red line runs through the roof space. It is a small structural tube that follows, in plan, the path of an arch; and the curve intersects the roof beams to pick up lateral loads being delivered along those lines. Two pairs of ties reach out to prevent the arch from buckling in its plane of action. As the lines of the structural system of arch and tie become interrupted by the beams, it is not clear what the thin red line means. Is it structure? Is it pattern? Or, is it architectural device? The answer is; all three.*
>
> *Structure need not be comprehensible and explicit. There is no creed or absolute that dictates structure must be recognized as a basic functional skeleton or the manifestation of a high-tech machine. It can be subtle and more revealing. It is a richer experience to my mind if a puzzle is set or a layer of ambiguity lies over the reading of 'structure'.*[14]

Other unconventional interior structure in the Kunsthal also expresses the ambiguity mentioned above. Chapter 2 discusses how the two lines

▲ **6.41** Front of the smaller lecture theatre.

▲ **6.42** Library, Delft Technical University, The Netherlands, Mecanoo Architekten, 1997. Sloping columns in the study-hall.

and the materiality of timber all combine to realize a warm, intimate and embracing space.

In most buildings, orthogonally configured structural members both respond to and express the rectilinear structural systems and architectural forms they support. Even when forms take on more complex geometries, primary structure usually maintains a rigid adherence to orthogonality. However, there are exceptions. The previous chapter explained how structure at the Delft Technical University library subdivided space within the main hall (see Fig. 5.22). There, ground floor columns express the geometry of the element they support by matching the inclination of the cone surface above. The same approach is repeated in a computer-equipped study hall whose north-facing wall leans inward (Fig. 6.42). Column spacing along the wall is reduced to half of that elsewhere in the hall, and this doubles the columns' visual presence. The result is a dramatic leaning colonnade that supports, expresses and visually heightens the slope of the glazed skin.

SUMMARY

Interior structure can transform otherwise nondescript interior spaces by contributing architectural qualities and character. This chapter presents three modes by which structure visually and conceptually enriches interior architecture — surface, spatial and expressive.

In the exploration of *surface* structure, the buildings discussed illustrate the architectural potential for enriching spaces using exposed structure located on interior surfaces. In several examples, quite elaborate structure creates attractive surface patterning. In others, exposure of structural elements that are normally concealed, coupled with a design approach characterized by simplicity and rigour, proves more than sufficient to transform spaces.

With respect to structure's *spatial* impacts, others have explained how structure generates a spatial field around it, affecting how a space is perceived and creating opportunities for 'place-making'. A simple study illustrates how, within the same volume, changes in structural layout can greatly affect how a space is read. Relatively small-scale structure that forms domestic-sized spatial units also affects our spatial experience. It instills an impression of being inhabited and of framing activities within it. Where larger in scale, interior structure offers many diverse spatial and visual experiences. At the extremes of structural scale, structure either all but disappears visually, or else its massiveness may be overwhelming. Structure also plays important roles ordering spaces, and in other cases, imposing a sense of spatial hierarchy.

The *expressive* potential of interior structure is boundless. The examples provided only begin to indicate the extent to which structure can express all manner of issues. Two structures illustrate expression of externally acting soil pressures. In another building, structure expresses concepts related to breaking conventions and 'the unexpected'. We also see structure mirroring the intensity of the emotional climate of one set of building occupants, and reassuring others in what could be termed 'a structural embrace'. Finally, interior structure can helpfully express and accentuate building geometries in such a way that leads to additional architectural enrichment.

REFERENCES AND NOTES

1   Cook, P. (1996). *Primer*. Academy Editions.
2   Cook (1996), p. 85.
3   Zerbst, R. (1991). *Antoni Gaudí*. Taschen, p. 115.
4   Ivy, R. A. (1992). *Fay Jones*. The American Institute of Architects Press, p. 35.
5   Brigatti, D. G. and Dahinden, J. (1997). *Spazi Evocanti il Mistero – la Chiesa S. Massimiliano Kolbe in Varese*. Grafiche Quirici, p. 114.
6   Pople, N. (2001). Caught in the web. *RIBA Journal*, Feb., pp. 37–44.
7   Ching, F. D. K. (1996). *Architecture: Form, Space & Order*, 2nd edn. John Wiley & Sons, p. 122.
8   Van Meiss, P. (1990). *Elements of Architecture: From Form to Place*. Van Nostrand Reinhold, p. 138.
9   Suckle, A. (1980). *By Their Own Design*. Whitney Library of Design, p. 14.
10 Abercrombie, S. (1983). Evaluation: Beaubourg already shows its years. *Architecture*, Sept., p. 70.
11 After Ogg, A. (1987). *Architecture in Steel: The Australian Context*. The Royal Australian Institute of Architects, p. 49.

12 Saint, A. (1991). Notre-Dame du Raincy. *The Architects' Journal*, 13 Feb., pp. 27–45.

13 See, for example, Frampton, K. (1995). *Studies in Tectonic Culture: The Poetics of Construction in Nineteenth and Twentieth Century Architecture.* Massachusetts Institute of Technology, p. 132.

14 Balmond, C. (2002). *informal.* Prestel, p. 64.

15 For a more detailed description of the system's complexity and action, refer to Addis, W. (2001). *Creativity and Innovation: The Structural Engineer's Contribution to Design.* Architectural Press, pp. 113–15.

16 Haward, B. (1989). Oxford University Museum. *The Architects' Journal*, 27 Sept., pp. 40–63.

7

Structural detailing

Introduction

Exposed structural detailing can contribute significantly to the architecture of a building. Detailing can transform ordinary or purely utilitarian structural members into objects of aesthetic delight, as well as communicating design ideas and concepts. This chapter begins by illustrating how architects express a wide diversity of design ideas through structural details. It then demonstrates the breadth of architectural qualities that detailing can contribute to designs, that in turn lead to aesthetically satisfying outcomes.

For the purposes of this discussion, structural detailing is understood as determining the form of and the shaping and finishing of structural members and their connections. Structural detailing, as a design process, comprises the design of the cross-section, elevational profile and the connections of a structural member in order to achieve the structural engineering requirements of stability, strength and stiffness. Detailing begins after the structural form for a given design is chosen. For example, if designers decide in principle to adopt an exposed timber post-and-beam system as shown in Fig. 7.1, they can select details from many possible combinations of differently detailed beams, columns, joints and finishes. A similar range of alternatives has been suggested for the detailing of structural steel members.[1]

The design concept should drive detailed design. Before attending to the specifics of structural details a designer should begin by revisiting his or her concept and interrogating it. How might it inform detailing decisions? Only then is it possible to achieve an architecture where all its structural members are integrated with all the other architectural elements and work together towards achieving the design concept. Such an outcome is improbable if a designer uncritically permits detailing choices to be constrained by typical or conventional practice. That will deny clients and building users opportunities for architectural enrichment. As Louis Khan writes:

> A building is like a human. An architect has the opportunity of creating life.
> It's like a human body – like your hand. The way the knuckles and joints

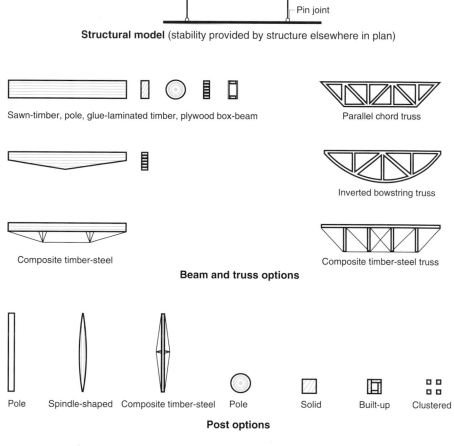

Structural model (stability provided by structure elsewhere in plan)

Pin joint

Sawn-timber, pole, glue-laminated timber, plywood box-beam

Parallel chord truss

Inverted bowstring truss

Composite timber-steel

Composite timber-steel truss

Beam and truss options

Pole   Spindle-shaped   Composite timber-steel   Pole   Solid   Built-up   Clustered

Post options

▲ **7.1**   Alternative structural member options for timber post-and-beam construction.

come together make each hand interesting and beautiful. In a building these details should not be put into a mitten and hidden. You should make the most of them. Space is architectural when the evidence of how it is made is seen and comprehended.[2]

Where detailing is hidden from view, however, then any design considerations beyond structural performance, economy and buildability are wasted. A pragmatic approach to detailing is quite sufficient.

As well as reflecting or expressing the architectural design concept, as noted above, structural detailing must be structurally adequate and consistent with the structural engineering assumptions. For example, a connection assumed pinned in the structural analysis should be detailed as such. Therefore, at least in buildings large enough to require professional structural engineering expertise, successful structural resolution, including detailing, requires close collaboration between architects and structural engineers. Structural detailing should therefore satisfy both the architectural design concept and structural necessity.

EXPRESSIVE AND RESPONSIVE DETAILING

Structural detailing expresses or responds to a wide variety of influences. In most cases, details are inspired by some aspect *within* the building being designed. Typical sources of inspiration include architectural form, function, materiality and construction, or structural actions. Examples of each are discussed in the following sections. Several buildings are then examined whose details reflect ideas or issues arising *outside* the building – perhaps an event, an aspect of technology, vernacular architecture, an aspect of culture or an historical period.

Architectural form

This detailing strategy adopts some feature of the architectural form to guide the development of structural details. If not laboured unduly, such an approach can bring a sense of harmony to a project, unifying otherwise possibly disparate elements. Where implemented successfully, the resulting details appear to have a sense of rightness or inevitability about them. As Architect Fay Jones, a widely acknowledged exponent of synthesizing the detail and the whole (architectural form) explains:

> *Organic architecture has a central generating idea; as in most organisms every part and every piece has a relationship. Each should benefit the other; there should be a family of form, and pattern. You should feel the relationship to the parts and the whole . . . The generating idea establishes the central characteristics, or the essence, or the nucleus, or the core; it's the seed idea that grows and generates the complete design, where it manifests itself from the large details down to the small subdivision of the details.*[3]

Two examples of structural details particularly well integrated with architectural form have already been mentioned briefly. In both, the detailing of the long-span vierendeel trusses at the Grande Arche (see Fig. 3.19), and the roof spine-beam at Saint Benedict Chapel (see Figs 6.4 and 6.5), detailing responds to form. Similarly well integrated relationships between structural detailing and architectural form are found at the Grand Louvre, Paris, and the Suhr office building.

In the underground foyer of the Louvre gallery, detailing of the coffered suspended ground floor slab reflects the precision and the geometrical

▲ **7.2**   Grand Louvre, Paris, France, I. M. Pei, 1989. Louvre pyramid.

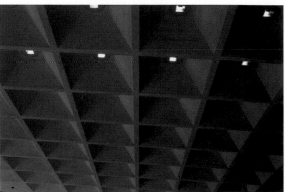

▲ **7.3**   Coffered slab soffit.

▲ **7.4**   Triangular recesses in the central column relate to the pyramid above.

▲ **7.5**   Suhr office building, Switzerland, Santiago Calatrava, 1985. The building is circular in plan, with an attached service core behind.

purity of the famous glazed pyramid above (Figs 7.2 and 7.3). The truncated pyramidal geometry of the coffer voids within the slab unifies the different construction materials through common forms. Detailing of the central column also exhibits the same theme of geometrical purity (Fig. 7.4). Full-height triangular incisions into each side of an otherwise square column, form a complex cross-section. The square and triangular shapes integrate with those of the coffers in the immediate vicinity, and with the pyramid above.

Structural detailing of the Suhr office building takes its cue from an essentially rounded floor plan (Fig. 7.5). Geometrically complex paddle-like

▲ 7.6   Perimeter blade-like pier.

▲ 7.7   Rounded precast concrete stair stringer.

ground floor piers approximate circular cross-sections at their bases and widen smoothly to become thin blades at their tops (Fig. 7.6). The main stairway, tucked into a service core behind the primary circular form, also incorporates rounded details. The rounded top and bottom surfaces of the precast concrete stringer are also consistent with the architectural form (Fig. 7.7).

Building function

In the following two examples, a commercial building and an art gallery, structural detailing both expresses and contributes positively to aspects of their functions. In the first case the detailing is highly refined, while in the second, it has been deliberately designed to appear relatively crude. Structural detailing responds to and reinforces the distinctive purpose of each building.

The Tobias Grau office and warehouse facility, Rellingen, illustrates a most appropriate relationship between detailing and building function (see Fig. 3.30). The company designs and manufactures high quality light-fittings which have been incorporated extensively into its new facilities. In this setting, structural detailing maintains an equivalently high aesthetic standard. The structural details are more readily comparable to those of furniture design than to typical building construction. The attractiveness of the main curved glue-laminated portal members is

▲ **7.12** United Airlines Terminal, Chicago, USA, Murphy/Jahn, 1987. The main concourse.

Materiality and construction

Some architecture is characterized by a strong expression of structural materiality and construction. Each structural material possesses features particular to its own materiality. For example, thinness of section, flanged cross-sectional shapes, potential for extreme slenderness in both compression and tension, and the ability to accommodate significant penetrations in members are characteristics unique to steel construction. Concrete, in a plastic or even completely fluid state while still fresh, can harden in moulds of almost any shape and display many different surface textures. Other signatures of concrete include negative details at construction joints and form-tie recesses. Timber materiality on the other hand is best expressed by its natural grain and colour, typical rectilinear cross-section shapes and connection details that respond to its relative softness and anisotropy. Certain structural configurations such as vertical and hierarchical layering of horizontal joists and beams, and relatively closely-spaced beams and posts are also trade-marks of timber construction.

This section, which illustrates structures whose detailing not only expresses building materiality and construction, but celebrates it, begins by considering a structural steel building whose materiality becomes apparent at first glance.

The structure of the United Airlines Terminal concourse and departure lounges, Chicago, utilizes a limited vocabulary of two steel sections, the I-beam and the tube (Figs 7.12 and 7.13). Highly penetrated I-beams form the irregularly shaped beams of portal frames that articulate and

▲ **7.13** Beam–column junction.

modulate the concourses. Tubes function as purlins and also as clustered columns for each portal-frame leg. In several spaces the two sections combine to form a composite beam with a conventional top I-beam flange but a tubular lower flange.

The architect has mostly used off-the-shelf sections, yet through varied structural form and consistent and refined detailing has facilitated a sense of liveliness, lightness and materiality. The high quality detailing of the exposed structure is largely responsible for this exemplary architecture that could have otherwise been a featureless and elongated space. A reviewer observes:

> Terminal 1 is not a project in which it is possible to hide a poor symbiosis of architecture and engineering disciplines; it is obvious that Jahn [the architect] and the structural engineers at Lev Zetlin Associates worked well together in an understanding of what the result should be. It has been noted that the structural expression so prevalent in the project – rounded forms, exposed ribs and structural members with punched webs – recalls the structural parts of aircraft; this layer of meaning, says Jahn, was unintentional . . . the assembly shows elegance in every detail. Steel connections and finishes could be the subject of a whole photographic essay in themselves. Joints, brackets, and end conditions have been taken past that point where they merely work, to become abstract sculpture.[5]

Exposed structural detailing also plays a dominant architectural role at Hazel Wood School, Southampton. Throughout the building, circular timber columns support a glue-laminated lattice roof (Fig. 7.14). While exhibiting the layering so typical of timber construction, the roof structure takes that characteristic a step further by interlacing the beam chords and spacing them apart by timber blocks in much the same way as at Westminster Lodge, Dorset (see Fig. 6.8). The transverse beams spanning the school hall read as vierendeel trusses. Additional structural layering occurs locally above the columns where short glue-laminated beams cantilever either side of column centrelines to receive loads from the two-way lattice beams. These beam-column details recall the timber brackets of vernacular Japanese construction (Fig. 7.15).

Whereas timber construction dominates the interior architecture of Hazel Wood School, concrete structure plays a similarly strong aesthetic role at the Benetton Communication Research Centre, FABRICA, Treviso. Exposed concrete dominates the interior of this almost entirely underground project. In typical Ando fashion the detailing expresses the construction process (Fig. 7.16). Precisely spaced form-tie recesses,

▲ **7.14** Hazel Wood School, Southampton, England, Hampshire County Council Architects Department, 1990. The hall roof structure is typical of that for the whole school.

▲ **7.15** Short beams transfer loads from the lattice roof to a column.

▲ **7.16** FABRICA (Benetton Communication Research Centre), Treviso, Italy, Tadao Ando & Associates, 2000. Concrete construction and materiality are clearly expressed in the structural elements defining the sunken courtyard.

precision alignment of formwork joints and a high standard of concrete finish reflect the care devoted to structural detailing. Surface finishing is especially important here because of the plainness of all other column and wall details.

By restricting himself to circular and rectangular formwork Ando does not exploit the plasticity of concrete like Santiago Calatrava. Several of his works, including the cast-in-place concrete Stadelhofen Railway Station underground mall, Zürich (see Fig. 7.51) and Satolas Railway Station, Lyons (see Fig. 8.9), display comprehensively the extent to which

▲ **7.18** Precast bracket and frame junction.

▲ **7.17** Ferry Terminal and office building, Hamburg, Germany, Alsop and Störmer, 1993. Partially exposed precast concrete A-frames.

concrete's materiality can be expressed. These buildings are essays in the architectural exploitation and expression of cast-in-place concrete as a structural material.

The typical characteristics of precast concrete – thin and compact cross-sections, relatively complex forms and repetitive member layout – are exemplified in the Ferry Terminal and office building, Hamburg (Fig. 7.17). Thirty-three pairs of precast concrete A-frames define the 200 m long building. Generally placed just inside the exterior skin on each side of the building, each pair of frames supports simply-supported beams and suspended floor slabs that span between them.

Several frame bases are exposed within the ferry terminal waiting-room. They support precast concrete cantilever brackets, similarly detailed as the main frames, to extend the terminal area beyond the main building line (Fig. 7.18). Given their skeletal form, blue painted finish and smallness of cross-section, the brackets could actually be mistaken for steel construction! The architect clearly articulates the pin connections between the A-frames and their brackets, and therefore emphasizes the site-jointed nature of the precast components. Both in their forms and connections, the brackets and frames are consistent with and expressive of the materiality of precast concrete.

The final two examples where structural materiality and construction are expressed clearly begin with the Guggenheim Museum, Bilbao. Just enough structure is exposed to explain the building's construction

▲ **7.19**   Guggenheim Museum, Bilbao, Spain, Frank O. Gehry & Associates, 1997. View of the museum from the Puente de La Salve bridge.

(Fig. 7.19). Although the structure of this remarkable building lies mainly hidden within its billowing and twisted sculptural forms, in several locations its skeletal steel structure is exposed. The most accessible and informative area of this exposure occurs at the tower (Fig. 7.20). In conjunction with the long gallery, the tower 'holds' the Puente de La Salve bridge to the main body of the museum. The exposed tower structure, visible from the bridge, explains how other building exterior surfaces are structured. Rather unexpectedly, a conceptually simple triangulated steel framework supports the geometrically complex skins. Compared to the audacious titanium clad three-dimensional curved surfaces, the adjacent structural details of nuts and bolts and standard steel sections appear quite crude. Their ordinariness disguises the extent of the underlying structural analytical and design sophistication.

On a far smaller scale, and more overtly than at Bilbao, Frank Gehry expresses the nuts and bolts of structure *inside* the Fisher Center, Annadale-on-Hudson, New York. Curved steel ribs and bent horizontal girts are the means of achieving the dramatic sculptural walls that form a protective skin around the main theatre (Figs 7.21 and 7.22). Steel I-sections, their flanges welded to curved web plates, rise from their foundations and span a four storey volume to gain support from the concrete walls that enclose the theatre. Braced within their planes, the entire construction of these ribbed walls – the inside surfaces of the stainless steel cladding sheets, the girts, ties, braces, cleats and even the

▲ **7.20**   The tower structure.

▲ **7.21**   Fisher Center, Bard College, Annadale-on-Hudson, New York, USA, Frank O. Gehry & Associates, 2002. Side elevation with the main entry canopy to the right.

heads of the self-tapping screws that connect the different components together, are exposed in a rare architectural move.

At the Carpentry Training School, Murau, exposure of structural detailing extends beyond 'informing' to 'educating' (Fig. 7.23). The timber roof structure can be envisaged playing an important pedagogical role in the life of the school – like the sprung-tensioned system of the Parisian civil engineering school (see Fig. 3.51). Given that the structural members of the workshop-spanning trusses are ordinary straight lengths of glue-laminated timber, their visually prominent connections awaken interest in structural detailing. The deep roof structure relies upon steel plates to join its timber members together. The plates, inserted into and fixed to the timber members by pressed-in steel dowels are then bolted together (Fig. 7.24).

Another more elegant detail, but less visible due to its height above ground, occurs at the level of clerestory glazing (Fig. 7.25). Stainless steel plates are bolted to timber studs to extend their height to eaves level. This unusual detail enables the combined timber–steel studs to span vertically between the floor slab and the roof diaphragm to which they transfer wind face-loads. Importantly, the detail expresses the fact that the exterior walls do not provide vertical support to the roof – the thin vertical plates are weak in compression. Under lateral loads, however, they bear horizontally against a steel rod that passes through their

▲ **7.22**   Exposed construction of an exterior wall that curves towards the theatre roof.

▲ **7.23**   Carpentry Training School, Murau, Austria, E. Giselbrecht, 1992. Rear elevation.

▲ **7.24**   Web members connect to a truss bottom-chord.

▲ **7.25**   Face-loads only are transferred through the plate-rod connection.

vertical slots. This detail simultaneously allows horizontal load transfer and unrestrained vertical movement between the plates and the roof structure.

Structural actions

Detailing that expresses structural actions within members and connections also provides opportunities for architectural enrichment. According to Collins, Soufflot, the eighteenth-century Rationalist architect who reacted against the ornamental embellishment of structural details, advocated 'simply limiting aesthetic effects to those which logically followed from the nature of the structural component, and designing those components in accordance with rational criteria'.[6] But the pendulum has swung since the 1700s. Now, architects such as Louis Kahn react against bland concrete and timber members muted by their rectilinearity in both cross-section and longitudinal elevation, and 'off-the-shelf' steel sections that satisfy nothing other than the outcome of engineering calculations. Referring to the pervasive use of steel I-beams, Khan criticized structural engineers who used excessive factors-of-safety in conjunction with steel beam standardization. In his view, this led to overly large member sizes 'and further limited the field of engineering expression stifling the creation of the more graceful forms which the stress diagrams indicated.'[7]

In the following examples where detailing expresses structural actions, including bending moment diagrams, two distinct types of expression may be found. In the first, detailing expresses the variation of structural actions, and nothing else. In the second type, to use Anderson's words, 'The functionally adequate form must be adapted so as to give expression to its function. The sense of bearing provided by the entasis of

▲ **7.26**   Jussieu University, Paris, France, Edouart Albert, 1965. Beam geometry expresses the bending moment diagram.

Greek columns became the touchstone of this concept . . .'[8] In other words, designers elaborate structural details in order to clarify the expression of structural action. First, then, unelaborated structural detailing.

The exposed first floor beams at Jussieu University, Paris, express their internal structural actions. Steel box-beams, curved both in elevation and plan, express the relative intensity of their bending moments (Fig. 7.26). The beams are simply supported and their elevational profiles take on the parabolic forms of their bending moment diagrams. One notes in passing that the architect has privileged the articulation of bending stress rather than shear stress. Shear stress, which usually increases linearly from a value of zero at a mid-span to reach its maximum value at the ends of a span, is rarely expressed. The suspended floor trusses at Centre Pompidou, Paris, are an exception (see Fig. 7.53). Their diagonal web members increase in diameter as they approach the truss supports in response to the increasing value of shear force.

By varying the beam flange-width in plan at the university, the beams narrow at their ends to match the diameter of the tubular-steel columns into which they frame. Such a high degree of column slenderness, given that the columns support five floors, indicates their inability to resist lateral loads and the necessity for the concrete structural cores elsewhere in the building plan to provide overall stability. The level of transparency provided by these small diameter columns is especially appreciated

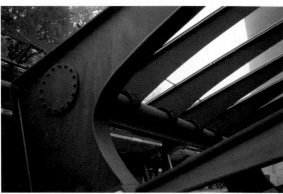

▲ **7.27**   Stadelhofen Railway Station, Zürich, Switzerland, Santiago Calatrava, 1990. Escalator entrance structure.

▲ **7.28**   Upper cantilever-to-torsion-beam connection, with smaller canopy cantilevers in the background.

given the 'sagging' beam profiles. Zannos suggests that designers should avoid this type of structural detailing:

> *If it is indeed true that we dislike forms that appear weak because their shape is deformed or seems to have been deformed by loading, it is quite natural that we prefer forms that are in contrast to that shape. We may thus propose the following law of aesthetics: a form . . . agrees with our aesthetic intuition – and, hence, satisfies us aesthetically – if its shape contrasts the shape that would have resulted if the form had been deformed by loading.*[9]

In this building, rather than the sagging beam soffits creating the sense of oppression that might be experienced in a more enclosed space, they lead the eye away from any potential visual heaviness towards the light and the open space on either side of the building.

The Stadelhofen Railway Station, Zürich, comprises a number of steel and concrete structures all of which to some degree illustrate detailing that expresses structural actions. For example, consider an escalator entrance structure (Fig. 7.27). The upper cantilever springs from a short pier bolted to a concrete base whose top surface slopes parallel with the cantilever. Immediately, by inclining its base Calatrava introduces a sense of dynamism to the structural form.

Like all other cantilever beams in the station, the cantilever tapers to a point, approximating the shape of its bending moment diagram. Near its end it supports an unusually configured and orientated two-pinned frame whose member profiles also match their bending moment diagrams. The form of this hanging lower structure recalls that of a swimmer diving. Under each of the two canopies of the escalator entrance, smaller beams cantilever from tubular torsion-resistant beams. The circular bolted plates express the transfer of torsion into the main members (Fig. 7.28). Here, detailing not only expresses structural actions

▲ **7.29** Stratford Regional Station, London, England, Wilkinson Eyre, 1999. Curved frames spring from cast-steel bases.

▲ **7.30** Lyons School of Architecture, France, Jourda et Perraudin, 1988. A cast-steel shoe expresses the compression load-path.

but its anthropomorphic forms create an aesthetic of movement and lightness.

At another railway station, the Stratford Regional Station, London, structural actions similarly inspire expressive detailing (Fig. 7.29). Although the focus here is upon just one detail, the base-connection of the portal frames, other details, such as how the primary curved frames taper to points where they are propped, equally express structural action. Each frame base-connection joins the frame rigidly to a concrete substructure. This base rigidity helps the frame resist gravity and lateral loads, and minimizes its depth.

High-strength bars tension the base-plates down to the concrete via cast-steel bases. Rather than adopt usual construction practice whereby a column base-plate connects directly to a concrete foundation by vertical bolts whose shafts are concealed, this detailing expresses how the base-plate is clamped down. Not only are the bolt shafts visible, but their inclination aligns them parallel to the lines of stress within the frame member. The shaping and roundness of the base exemplifies the 'adapting' of form, spoken of by Anderson previously. The base expresses and elaborates how tensions from the embedded bars compress the base-plate against the concrete, and how this compression stress that acts upon the base is dispersed uniformly at the steel-base to concrete interface.

Connections of timber members at the Lyons School of Architecture, Lyons, present a more overt example of elaborating structural details for the sake of improved expression (see Fig. 6.17). Delicate cast-steel shoes provide the transition detail at both ends of the inclined struts and vertical columns (Fig. 7.30). The elaboration of these details takes the form of four ribs that fan out from the steel-pin housing, and spread over the member depth, expressing the flow of compression force just as effectively as do the attached shafts of Gothic piers. The ribs illustrate how force is transferred from a relatively large and soft timber cross-section and channelled into a far smaller and harder steel pin.

The detail is adapted for beam-column connections, although the expression of (shear) force flowing from beam to column through the castings is less obvious (Fig. 7.31). What *is* clear however is an expression of clamping action – of the timber beam being clamped between castings that are fixed to the timber by screws top and bottom. Rather than expressing load paths, the clamping nature of the connection mechanism is communicated visually. This detail is a reminder of Chernikhov's seven constructivist joints, each of which expresses a different nature of connection.[10] Before leaving this junction, note that its unusual form allows a down-pipe to pass through it, just millimetres from the end of the beam. This is a simple example of how the necessity for structure and services integration frequently gives rise to inventive and expressive structural forms and details.[11]

The final example where detailing is inspired by some feature inherent in the building, expresses another form of connectivity – clasping. An oriel on the main façade of Palau Güell, Barcelona, projects over the street and is supported underneath by short cantilevers (Fig. 7.32). Their rounded profiles are mirrored by a row of similar cantilevers above the roof. Both sets of cantilevers appear to be doing more than just supporting gravity loads. Their tips wrap around and against the horizontal slabs as if to prevent them from sliding towards the street. Taking the form of bent fingers holding a cell-phone in the hand, they

▲ **7.31** A beam-column connection where a horizontal gap between the castings allows for a down-pipe to pass through the detail where required.

▲ **7.32** Palau Güell, Barcelona, Spain, Antonio Gaudí, 1880. Cantilevering brackets clasp the oriel floor.

read as clasps – like those restraining jewels in their settings, holding the oriel against the main building.

Other sources of inspiration

To conclude this study of expressive and responsive detailing, three examples are noted where structural details are inspired by sources from outside the building or its programme. First, the eclectic structural detailing of the Glasgow School of Art roof structures, where above the main stair and surrounding exhibition space, decorative timber trusses evoke images of medieval construction (Fig. 7.33). In another space, a roof bracket detail indicates a Japanese influence (Fig. 7.34).

At the post-modern Staatsgalerie, Stuttgart, structural details also draw upon a diverse range of external sources (Figs 7.35 and 7.36). The

▲ **7.33** Glasgow School of Art, Scotland, Charles Rennie Mackintosh, 1899. Truss forms inspired by medieval construction.

▲ **7.34** An elaborate roof-beam bracket.

▲ **7.35** Staatsgalerie, Stuttgart, Germany, James Stirling, Wilford & Associates, 1984. A classically detailed structure frames an entrance.

▲ **7.36** Mushroom reinforced concrete columns in a gallery.

columns and lintel that frame an exterior entrance, clearly express their classical origins. Inside the building, concrete mushroom columns are exposed in several spaces. They evoke images of the flat-slab columns that were introduced in the early 1900s, and in particular, those columns that support the roof of Frank Lloyd Wright's 1930s Johnson Wax administration building, Racine, Wisconsin.

Rather than drawing upon historical sources to inform the detailing of the Beehive, Culver City, California, the architect explores ideas of 'balanced unbalance'.[12] At ground floor the structural form is as unusual as the structural detailing above. Four square hollow-section posts that appear to be haphazardly orientated in plan and section lean outwards and are wrapped around horizontally by regularly spaced steel pipes that generate the curved form akin to an inverted beehive (Fig. 7.37). At first floor one encounters most unconventional structural detailing. The two rear posts kink as in a knee-joint, but the detailing suggests that the structure has snapped in bending. The rotation at each joint is expressed graphically by a triangular 'crack' or gap between the upper and lower sections of the posts (Fig. 7.38). Notions of instability, fragility and damage are conjured up in one's mind. Only upon closer inspection one sees how welded steel plates within the hollow sections provide enough strength for structural safety.

▲ **7.37** The Beehive, Culver City, USA, Eric Owen Moss Architects, 2001. The exterior with the main entrance to the left.

▲ **7.38** A 'broken' post at first-floor level.

AESTHETIC QUALITIES OF DETAILING

Introduction

This section explores and illustrates the enormous diversity of the aesthetic qualities of structural detailing. Pairs of contrasting qualities are categorized into four broad groupings. The process of categorization is imprecise since some details can be discussed in the context of another grouping. But the purpose is not to pigeon-hole a detail aesthetically, but rather to illustrate the amazing variety of different structural languages and approaches to structural detailing. Each detail invites its own architectural reading and influences how building users perceive and experience the architecture of which it is part.

Refined to utilitarian

Although one might expect refined structural detailing in all works of architecture, this certainly is not the case. Sometimes the budget or time constraints frustrate opportunities for refinement. Perhaps to ensure consistency with an architectural concept that for example requires a raw industrial aesthetic, refinement is avoided deliberately.

Refined structural details are frequently described by such terms as pure and elegant. Any extraneous material and componentry has been edited away. One is left with the impression that the detail cannot be improved upon. It has undergone an extensive process of reworking that has left the designer satisfied with the outcome – the technical and aesthetic requirements resolved in a synthesis of structural necessity and artistic sensibility.

Beginning with two examples of refined detailing, readers will recall that the expression of architectural quality on the exterior of Bracken House, London, has already been discussed and some of its exposed details noted (see Figs 4.40 and 4.41). The building's exterior provides other examples of refined detailing, such as on the main entrance truss that supports a translucent canopy (Figs 7.39 and 7.40). Metal bosses articulate the joints between the bottom-chord members and the others that are inclined. The spoke-like diagonals, ribbed and tapered to match the structural dimensions at each end, possess the same visual qualities as elegant mechanical or aeronautical engineering components.

A similar high degree of structural detailing refinement is evident at Queen's Building, Cambridge (Fig. 7.41). In describing it, a reviewer observes: 'One would say that the building was a montage of Hopkins motifs, were it not such a unified, monolithic form – more like a beautifully crafted piece of furniture than a building.'[13] The composite timber and stainless-steel theatre roof trusses incorporate refined structural

▲ **7.39**   Bracken House, London, England, Michael Hopkins and Partners, 1991. Main entrance canopy.

▲ **7.40**   Refined truss members.

▲ **7.41**   Queen's Building, Cambridge, England, Michael Hopkins and Partners, 1995. Main façade.

details (Fig. 7.42). Precisely located bolts pass through stainless-steel plates inserted between timber members. Rods elegantly connect to and fan out from a plate at a truss apex. The building exterior also features notable exposed structural detailing. Small stainless-steel ring-nodes denote the anchorages of an innovative post-tensioning system

▲ **7.42** Refined roof truss detailing.

▲ **7.43** A post-tensioning node detail.

▲ **7.44** School of Architecture, Marne-la-Vallée, Paris, France, Bernard Tschumi, 1999. Looking towards the main entrance.

▲ **7.45** Unrefined steel beams pass over a work-space atop the lecture block inserted into the atrium.

that reinforces the solid limestone masonry piers (Fig. 7.43). Specially selected aggregates for the concrete blocks housing the nodes match the colour of the surrounding stone blocks.

The School of Architecture, Marne-la-Vallée, Paris, illustrates less refined detailing (Figs 7.44 and 7.45). An industrial quality pervades the all-concrete-and-steel exposed structure. Consider the four steel beams that span an internal atrium, partially occupied by a box-like lecture theatre. Their unrefined cross-sections and longitudinal profiles raise questions such as why their shapes have not been better integrated with the saw-tooth roof form? However, this beam detailing *is* consistent with the basic quality of exposed steelwork elsewhere whose galvanized surfaces are left unpainted. The standard of detailing

▲ **7.46**   Attic conversion, Vienna, Austria, Coop Himmelb(l)au, 1988. The attic roof over-sails the existing building.

▲ **7.47**   Irregularity of the form is reflected in the detailing.

is totally compatible with the architect's concept: 'It's never a closed system . . . You never contain it. You always leave gaps, interstices. It's never about synthesis. It's always about certain fractures. So the fractures are generally all intentional. It's not like Norman Foster who will always try to close the system. I always try to leave it open.'[14]

In contrast to the refined structural detailing of Bracken House and Queen's Building and the more basic detailing of the School of Architecture, raw and irregular details characterize the Attic conversion, Vienna (Figs 7.46 and 7.47). Such a deliberate lack of refinement again seems quite appropriate within a chaotic structural assemblage described variously as 'an eagle', 'a crazy composition', 'a snapshot of a disastrous collision' and 'a constructional thunderstorm'! Details therefore mirror the general absence of structural rationality. Their random and fractured qualities verge on the crude.

Simple to complex

This grouping of aesthetic qualities is not intended to imply an absence of refinement, and in fact, both the following examples illustrate refinement in different ways. At the Millennium Seed Bank, Sussex, details have been pared down to the bare minimum (Figs 7.48 and 7.49). A 'less is more' approach complements the simple barrel-vaulted and frame forms. This simple and restful architecture achieves the architect's design concept to 'evoke a sense of spirituality and create a space for private reflection where both adult and child should leave feeling enriched.'[15]

Conversely, the Louvre Pyramid, Paris (see Fig. 7.2) illustrates complex detailing. Although a simple architectural form, an aspiration for

▲ **7.48** Millennium Seed Bank, Wakehurst Place, Sussex, England, Stanton Williams, 2000. Barrel-vaulted roof forms.

▲ **7.49** Detailing matches the simple structural forms.

▲ **7.50** Grand Louvre, Paris, France, I. M. Pei, 1989. Visually confusing structure.

transparency has led to structural complexity. Rather than frame the pyramid conventionally with solid sloping rafters spanning between the base and the four ridges of the pyramid, the architect opted for a diagonally orientated system – a two-way grillage of stressed cable-beams. While small diameter stainless-steel members offer a high degree of transparency, from many viewing angles the profusion of rods and connections is visually confusing (Fig. 7.50). Visual complexity arises primarily due to the large number of individual members, even though each is small.

▲ **7.51**   Stadelhofen Railway Station, Zürich, Switzerland, Santiago Calatrava, 1990. Cambering the beams and the 'sloping columns' visually lighten the shopping mall.

Lightness to heaviness

Designers often seek to maximize ingress of natural light and achieve a high degree of transparency in external walls as discussed more extensively in Chapter 8. They usually adopt a strategy entailing many slender, rather than fewer larger members. As noted at the Louvre pyramid, while structure might exhibit acceptable qualities of lightness and transparency, from some viewpoints its appearance is less successful. It is important to remember that people mostly view and experience structure from positions other than those used to generate plans, sections and elevations.

Sensitivity to human proximity also motivates a lightness of touch in detailing. Visual harshness of members and perceptions of size can be relieved by introducing curved surfaces, as in the subterranean Museum of Gallo-Roman Civilization, Lyons (see Figs 6.30 and 6.31). Chamfering the lower third of the deep beams and the smooth curved transitions between the columns and beams softens their visual impact and renders the structure less formidable. Rounded surfaces incorporated into the precast concrete floor units also 'soften' the concrete soffits and achieve an attractive textured ceiling. Concrete surfaces can also be 'softened' in a tactile and visual sense by sandblasting, as in the Cambridge Law Faculty Building, Cambridge (see Fig. 7.61), or by light bush-hammering.

The Stadelhofen Railway Station underground mall, Zürich, also exemplifies detailing that visually lightens otherwise large concrete members (Figs 7.51 and 7.52). Pier detailing incorporates two setbacks in plan

▲ **7.52**   Pier detailing.

▲ **7.53**   Centre Pompidou, Paris, France, Piano and Rogers, 1977. Double-chords reduce the visual mass of the truss.

▲ **7.54**   Institut du Monde Arabe, Paris, France, Jean Nouvel, 1987. Light vierendeel trusses support the end wall.

that reduces its visual mass and scale, rendering the space more amenable to human habitation. The thinnest portion of a pier cross-section when traced from its base up to the beam and down to the base of the opposite pier reads as a portal frame. The next thicker area appears to be supporting and connected to the keel-like ceiling shape, and the thickest remaining section is seen as part of the walls above the shop frontages. Structural details like these downsize one's perception of structure towards human-scale and create friendlier, more humane environments.

Use of multiple members is another strategy to prevent people from feeling overwhelmed by otherwise large structural elements. The double-chords of the Pompidou Centre trusses, Paris, have their visual mass reduced to a minimum (Fig. 7.53 and see Fig. 4.18), and the clustered columns of the United Airlines Terminal have a similar effect (see Fig. 7.13). Multiplicity of structural members may bring additional aesthetic benefits as well, such as introducing a sense of rhythm to an elevation or a space.

Returning to lightness of detailing for transparency, L'Institut du Monde Arabe, Paris, illustrates in at least two areas a successful detailing strategy utilizing composite rather than solid members. Open vierendeel box-trusses span the width of the narrow exterior wall of the main façade (Fig. 7.54). Positioned in front of the cladding, they offer support to it at each floor level. With their outer chords curved in plan, they

▲ **7.55**   Internal horizontal trusses in the library.

contribute a diaphanous softness to the façade. Other internal box trusses support the skin in double-height spaces such as the library. But these are detailed completely differently. Diagonal web members, together with four parallel tubular chords, achieve new qualities of intricacy and ornateness (Fig. 7.55). Their transparency and visual complexity compliment similar qualities present in the glazed and mechanically shuttered curtain-walls. It is worth reflecting on how greatly the aesthetic qualities of the space would change if the existing trusses were replaced by solid box or tubular-beams.

Another example of structural detailing for lightness can be observed in Charles de Gaulle Airport, Terminal 2F, Paris. Whereas in the first visit to the building it was noted how the massive exterior structure signalled entry (see Fig. 4.30), now the structural lightness inside the terminal is experienced. A 200 m long 'peninsula' that houses departure lounges and aircraft walkways juts out from the air-side of the main terminal building. A series of transverse portal frames whose detailing is so 'light' that the whole structure almost reads as a space frame, supports its roof (Figs 7.56 and 7.57). Structural detailing is not locked into an orthogonal grid but responds to the roof form that appears like an upturned boat hull. The truss nodes map the gently curving roof contours, and via innovative light-weight tension-spokes, the trusses wrap around and under the floor slab. The structure delivers a light-filled space while displaying a remarkable degree of lightness. Compared to the heaviness of the terminal land-side concrete wall and ceiling surfaces, this air-side structure looks as if it could take off!

▲ **7.56**   Charles de Gaulle Airport: Terminal 2F, Paris, France, Aéroports de Paris, 1999. Light-weight 'peninsula' roof.

▲ **7.57**   Tension-spokes allow frames to wrap around the floor slab.

▲ **7.58**   Learning Resource Centre, Thames Valley University, Slough, England, Richard Rogers Partnership, 1996. The two exterior forms.

In the progression towards examples of visually heavier detailing two buildings are visited that incorporate instances of both light and heavy detailing. The Learning Resource Centre, Slough, consists of three forms – a main rectilinear concrete-framed block housing bookcases, seminar rooms and offices; a light-weight curved roof enclosing a three-storey volume; and within it, a single-storey concrete structure whose upper floor accommodates computing and study areas (Fig. 7.58).

Detailing for lightness is most evident in the curved roof structure, although vertical posts at each end of the light-weight structure are

▲ **7.60** Faculty of Law Building, Cambridge, England, Sir Norman Foster and Partners, 1996. The light-weight façade structure contrasts with the concrete columns.

▲ **7.59** Lightened by the use of tension-ties, the curved beams arch over a computing area.

▲ **7.61** Raking concrete columns with a 'softening' sand-blasted finish.

generously penetrated. The curved primary beam depths are kept to a minimum. Ties that connect to intermediate points along the beams effectively deepen them structurally without increasing their visual mass (Fig. 7.59). Beam legibility, already reinforced by a bright yellow finish, is further enhanced by concealing roof purlins behind the perforated ceiling cladding. The typically dimensioned solid beam and column members of the reinforced concrete frames provide the contrasting heavy detailing.

The Faculty of Law Building, Cambridge, also illustrates both light and heavy detailing (Fig. 7.60). Curved vierendeel trusses form a triangulated-lattice vault structure to the fully glazed north-facing wall. Springing from ground level and propped horizontally at third floor level, the vault rises another two storeys to curve back to a line of support towards the far side of the building. The vault structural members are so much lighter than the substantial raking columns that support approximately half the total floor area of the building (Fig. 7.61).

Examples of exposed structure that are detailed to accentuate a sense of heaviness rather than lightness are rare in contemporary buildings given a general preoccupation with transparency and its offer of light and views. The chunkiness evident in some contemporary footwear and motor vehicles is yet to find wide acceptance architecturally. The visually heavy structural detailing at the Centre for Understanding the

▲ **7.62** Centre for Understanding the Environment (CUE), Horniman Museum, London, England, Architype, 1997. Front façade with chimney-columns.

Environment (CUE), London, is a consequence of its ecologically sustainable design, rather than any other reason. Primary structural members are hollow, exemplifying the highest possible level of structure and services integration (Figs 7.62 and 7.63).[16] Structural members function as air conduits in this naturally ventilated building. Column and beam cross-sections are therefore larger than expected for a building essentially of domestic scale, even accounting for the weight of its turf roof. Warm air is extracted through circular penetrations in the triangular cross-section plywood web-beams, and channelled horizontally to columns. Columns that terminate above roof height as chimneys, move air vertically. For such a relatively small building the structural members appear heavy.

Plain to decorative

LaVine describes the exterior ground floor columns of the iconic Villa Savoye, Paris (Figs 7.64 and 7.65), as 'classically placed but unadorned, slender cylinders, reflecting a technological stance of the twentieth century'.[17] Consistent with the plainness of the columns, the floor beams are rectangular in both cross-section and elevation. Their widths that equal the diameters of the columns and result in tidy beam–column junctions, are evidence of attention to detailing that does not seek attention.

A more recent building illustrates the potential for structural detailing with decorative qualities to enhance architecture. The ribbed concrete

▲ **7.63** Interior column and beam.

▲ **7.64** Villa Savoye, Paris, France, Le Corbusier, 1929. The front and a side elevation.

▲ **7.65** Plain exterior column and beam detailing.

▲ **7.66** Schlumberger Extension building, Cambridge, England, Michael Hopkins and Partners, 1992. Exposed ribbed soffits around the perimeter.

floor soffits of the Schlumberger Extension building, Cambridge, are reminiscent of the isostatic ribs indicating lines of constant stress in the concrete slabs designed by Pier Luigi Nervi in the 1950s (Fig. 7.66). Floor construction at Cambridge was achieved using permanent ferrocement formwork, subsequently infilled with reinforced concrete. Continuing the ribbed theme on the façade that is achieved by the closely spaced tubular columns, the sculptural qualities of the concrete ribs enrich the visual appearance of the cantilevering soffit.

The exquisitely detailed wrought-iron beams of the Bibliothèque Sainte-Geneviève, Paris, also provide a fine example of decorative structural detailing (Fig. 7.67). A flowing pattern resembling stars and sickles replaces the standard diagonal web members that usually join top and bottom chords. Here, structural detailing and artistry merge in these much admired members.

The Hamburg Museum Courtyard Canopy, Hamburg, provides the final example of decorative structural detailing. A fully glazed grid-shell structure roofs an L-shaped courtyard (Fig. 7.68). Pairs of 6 mm diameter pre-tensioned cables form a triangular mesh to stiffen the orthogonal grid, fabricated from 60 mm by 40 mm steel section. Commenting upon the architectural qualities of the canopy, Holgate explains:

> The problem of diagonal bracing members competing for visual interest with those of an orthogonal grid has been solved by the lightness of the prestressed cables which here form a delicate accompaniment to the stronger lines of the steel slats. As usual, much thought has been given to the details both from an architectural and technical standpoint. These are an essential element in the success of the roof. The project is an excellent

▲ **7.67** Bibliothèque Sainte-Geneviève, Paris, France, Henri Labrouste, 1850. Curved iron beams over the reading room.

outcome of the quest for lightness, delicacy, minimalism, and unobtrusiveness in structure.[18]

While the designers tried to minimize the visual impact of most details, one in particular stands out. In three locations, and most importantly where the two arms of the L-shape meet in the corner and the roof bulges beyond its normal barrel forms, additional tensile stiffening maintains the cylindrical geometry. Vertical fans of cables radiate upwards from a central plate suspended high above the courtyard floor and held in physical and visual equilibrium by an inverted V-shaped tension cable. A stainless-steel plate whose roundedness echoes that of the vaulted form above, its shininess, the fan-like layout of cables and intricacy of connectors between plate and lower cable, all create an impression of a necklace-like piece of jewellery (Fig. 7.69).

SUMMARY

Having defined structural detailing as the configuration, shaping and finishing of members and their connections, the chapter explores how detailing makes significant architectural contributions to buildings.

First, it examines the expressive and responsive nature of structural detailing. An analysis of observed structural details suggests that most express or respond to some aspect of the building of which they are part. Examples illustrate details that relate to architectural form, building function, materiality and construction, and structural actions.

▲ **7.68** Hamburg Museum Courtyard Canopy, Hamburg, Germany, Von Gerkan, Marg and Partner, 1989. General view of the canopy.

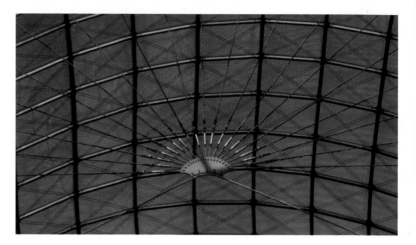

▲ **7.69**   The fan detail possesses the aesthetic qualities of a piece of jewellery.

Detailing that expresses structural actions can either express bending or other stress, or articulate structural connectivity like clamping or clasping. Some sources of detailing inspiration lie completely outside the building and its programme.

The second and final section of the chapter illustrates the huge diversity of the aesthetic qualities of structural detailing. Each detail suggests its own architectural reading and influences its surrounding architecture. Detailing qualities are categorized into the following four broad groupings – refined to utilitarian, simple to complex, lightness to heaviness, and plain to decorative.

The multiplicity of examples, the sheer diversity of expressive and responsive details, and the different aesthetic qualities of details indicate the enormous potential for exposed structural detailing to enhance the realization of architectural concepts.

REFERENCES AND NOTES

1   Ogg, A. (1987). *Architecture in Steel: The Australian Context.* The Royal Australian Institute of Architects, p. 44.

2   Louis Khan, quoted in Frampton, K. (1995). *Studies in Tectonic Culture: The Poetics of Construction in Nineteenth and Twentieth Century Architecture.* Massachusetts Institute of Technology, p. 227.

3   Jones, F. (1999). '*Outside the Pale': The Architecture of Fay Jones.* Department of Arkansas Heritage, pp. 48 and 54.

4   Balmond, C. (2002). *informal.* Prestel, p. 88.

5   Murphy, J. (1987). A Grand Gateway. *Progessive Architecture,* Nov., pp. 95–104.

6 Collins, P. (1998). *Changing Ideals in Modern Architecture 1750–1950*, 2nd edn. McGill–Queens University Press, p. 127.

7 Louis Khan, quoted in Frampton, K. (1995). *Studies in Tectonic Culture: The Poetics of Construction in Nineteenth and Twentieth Century Architecture.* Massachusetts Institute of Technology, p. 210.

8 Anderson, quoted in the essay 'Towards a Critical Regionalism: Six Points for an Architecture of Resistance', in Frampton, K. (2002). *Labour, Work and Architecture: Collected Essays on Architecture and Design.* Phaidon, p. 88.

9 Zannos, A. (1987). *Form and Structure in Architecture: The Role of Statical Function.* Van Nostrand Reinhold, p. 162.

10 Joint types of penetration, clamping, embracing, mounting, interfacing, coupling and integration are defined and discussed in Reno, J. (1992). Constructing beginnings: a role for building technology in architectural design education. *Journal of Architectural Education*, 45 (3), May, pp. 161–70.

11 Charleson, A. W. (1998). Aesthetics of architectural structural and services integration. *Proceedings of the 32nd Annual Conference of the Australia and New Zealand Architectural Science Association*, 15–17 July, pp. 145–50.

12 Hutt, D. (2002). In Culver City, California, Eric Owen Moss builds the Beehive – a playfully sculptural structure and a creative workplace abuzz with activity. *Architectural Record*, 08:02, pp. 130–5.

13 Davies, C. (1996). Cambridge credo. *Architectural Review*, 199 (1188), pp. 47–51.

14 Quoted in Such, R. (2000). So Tschumi. *World Architecture*, 84, pp. 40–4.

15 Bevan, R. (2000). Seed Capital. *Building Design*, Oct. 27, pp. 17–19.

16 For a ranking of levels of structure and services integration refer to Rush, R. D. (1986). *The Building Systems Integration Handbook.* The American Institute of Architects/John Wiley & Sons, p. 12.

17 LaVine, V. (2001). *Mechanics and Meaning in Architecture.* University of Minnesota Press, p. 163.

18 Holgate, A. (1997). *The Art of Structural Engineering: The Work of Jorg Schlaich and His Team.* Edition Axel Menges, p. 114.

8

STRUCTURE AND LIGHT

INTRODUCTION

Following the view that architectural space exists when it is experienced by the senses, particularly sight, Van Meiss considers architectural design to be 'the art of placing and controlling light sources in space'.[1] He understands light sources to include actual light sources such as windows as well as illuminated objects like enclosing surfaces or other architectural elements that could include structural members. From this perspective, structure is potentially an important architectural element – both as a source of light, where light passes through it or illuminates it, and also as controller of how and where light enters a space.

When stone and masonry load-bearing wall construction dominated previous periods of architectural history, openings for light could be considered the absence of structure. Millet's description of the relationship between structure and light is particularly applicable to that former era. Focusing more on structure's potential to control light than function as a source of light itself, she writes: 'Structure defines the place where light enters. The structural module provides the rhythm of light, no light. Where the structure is, there is no light. Between the structural elements there is light.'[2] However, since the introduction of metal skeletal structural forms during the nineteenth century, it is no longer a case of either structure or light in architectural space – both can co-exist. Slender structural members have a minimal impact upon the amount of light entering a space. Whereas the former prevalence of masonry structure, in plan and elevation necessitated its penetration in order to introduce light, in current architectural practice daylight requirements frequently determine structural form and detailing. Contemporary structure with its relative slenderness and small plan 'footprint' can usually meet these demands.

Depending upon its configuration, structure either inhibits or facilitates the ingress of light. In a building with perimeter structure that does not exclude natural light, structure relates to light in one of four modes – as a source of light where, for example, light passes through a roof truss to enter a space; to maximize light by minimizing the shadow effect of

▲ **8.2** San Francisco International Airport, USA, Skidmore Owings & Merrill LLP, 2000. A two-dimensional truss transforms into three dimensions over the central span of the terminal.

▲ **8.3** Light passing through a three-dimensional truss.

▲ **8.4** Dome Leisure Centre, Doncaster, England, FaulknerBrowns Architects, 1989. A glazed truss-to-column connection.

At the Dome Leisure Centre, Doncaster, triangular roof trusses project above the roof plane that attaches to the truss bottom-chords (Fig. 8.4). Where the trusses are glazed, their sloping sides function as strip skylights. The Carpentry Training School, Murau, displays a similar approach (see Fig. 7.23). Here the roof plane meets the primary truss half-way between the top and bottom-chords. The top half of the sloping sides of the truss are glazed and light also enters from perimeter clerestory glazing.

A stepped roof form at the Kew Swimming and Recreation Centre, Melbourne, provides another alternative to conventional surface-mounted light sources such as roof skylights. The step in the roof becomes a near-vertical glazed surface and creates a more interesting exterior form and interior space compared to a horizontal roof and skylight (Fig. 8.5). In this building the truss depth rather than its width determines daylighting levels. Natural light passes through the truss that spans the length of the building, into the main pool area. Given its overall lightness, the fineness of its members and their tubular form and neatly welded joints, the truss itself is an attractive architectural element.

Structure also acts as a light source, albeit infrequently, where light passes through an area of structure normally regarded, at least by structural engineers, as a critical joint region. The Baumschulenweg Crematorium,

▲ **8.5** Kew Swimming and Recreation Centre, Melbourne, Australia, Daryl Jackson Architects, 1990. Light penetrates the truss that defines the step in the roof.

▲ **8.6** Sant Jordi Sports Hall, Barcelona, Spain, Arata Izosaki & Associates, 1990. Light enters through constructional fold-line joints, as in this corner of the roof structure.

Berlin, where light audaciously enters the condolence hall through annuli at the column to roof-plate junctions and the longitudinal wall to roof connections, has already been visited. Both structural junctions, usually important from the perspective of gravity and lateral loads have had their load transfer mechanisms modified for the sake of light (see Figs 2.14 and 2.15).

Other cases of light passing through structural joints are exemplified in two sporting facilities. At the Stellingen Ice Skating Rink, Hamburg, mentioned previously, areas in the vicinity of the fabric and its supports are well suited for introducing light. The need for the fabric–steel interfaces to be dispersed in order to avoid puncturing or tearing the highly stressed fabric, rather than be concentrated, provides such an opportunity (see Fig. 8.1).

In the second example, light passes through joints into the Sant Jordi Sports Hall roof, Barcelona (Fig. 8.6). The unique feature of these joints is that they express the hinge or fold-lines necessitated by the Pantadome System of roof erection. In this construction method the roof structure is first assembled on the ground and then raised by hydraulic jacks. As the roof rises, hinges allow the central dome and peripheral areas to fold relative to each other, and when the roof is in its final position, additional structural members lock the hinge zones to stabilize the structure before de-propping.[8] Although many small skylights over the central dome also contribute to the lighting levels, the temporary hinged-joint regions are the primary light sources.

While designers arrange for light to pass through open structural systems or connections between structural members, most light enters a

▲ **8.7**   Burrell Gallery, Glasgow, Scotland, Barry Gasson Architects, 1983. Repetitive yet attractive glass and timber restaurant enclosure.

▲ **8.8**   Portuguese Pavilion, Lisbon, Portugal, Alvaro Siza, 1998. Light passes through the slit in the concrete slab and between the stainless-steel tendons.

building through penetrations in the external walls and roof cladding. These are usually positioned and shaped to respect the layout and geometry of the underlying supporting structure. Windows and sky-lights are normally positioned between structural members. The Burrell Gallery restaurant, Glasgow – a timber and glass 'lean-to' that wraps around the south-east corner of the gallery – provides a simple yet attractive example (Fig. 8.7). Natural light entering the fully glazed enclosure passes between closely spaced 330 mm by 100 mm glue-laminated timber posts and rafters. While a strong yet simple rhythm of structure and light characterizes the space, structure not only limits the daylight, but to some extent modifies it. Given that the posts and rafters are spaced at little more than twice their depths, the members create shade and also reflect light off their vertical surfaces.

Light passes between the structural members of the reinforced con-crete catenary of the Portuguese Pavilion, Lisbon, far more dramatically (see Fig. 3.9). An unprecedented design decision led to the removal of a narrow strip of concrete at the northern end of the catenary that would normally cover the tension rods. Above the podium where visit-ing dignitaries to Expo '98 were publicly welcomed, sunlight filters through exposed stainless-steel rods. Striated shadows pattern the but-tress walls that withstand the catenary tensions (Fig. 8.8). The project structural engineer, Cecil Balmond, describes the effect poetically:

> *Made out of concrete, the curve flies seventy metres without apparent effort – from afar it looks as if it is made of paper. And at the last moment of span, just before the safety of the vertical anchors, the form is cut. Lines of cables cross the void instead, pinning themselves to strong abutments.*

▲ **8.9** Railway Station at Satolas Airport, Lyons, France, Santiago Calatrava, 1994. Glazing centred over the main concourse.

▲ **8.10** A view across the concourse. Glazed areas are integrated with the pattern of ribs.

This de-materialisation is both a denial and a release. Weight vanishes and the mass hovers. Like the underbelly of some flying saucer the canopy floats. It is a trick of the light.[9]

The railway station at Satolas Airport, Lyons, is the final example where structure defines the extent of penetrations for natural light. Two rows of skylights run the length of the train platforms. Each diamond-shaped area of glazing reflects the geometrical pattern of the underlying structural ribs (Figs 8.9 and 8.10) In section, structure reads as a series of portal frames, but not of the type found in most buildings. Each frame, skewed to the main axis, expresses a sense of lightness and elegance with its outwardly inclined columns and cambered beams. The intersections and bifurcations of the frames create the attractive and flowing skeletal framework into which the skylights are so well integrated.

The Satolas Airport structure also integrates artificial lighting effectively – in a far more sophisticated manner than merely providing a means of support for surface-mounted or hung light-fittings. Lights that illuminate the ribs soaring over the outer two station platforms are recessed within sculptured stub-columns (Fig. 8.11). Located between the perimeter diagonal struts and the roof ribs the lighting details recall Calatrava's similar but less ghoulish integration of structure and artificial light at the Stadelhofen Railway Station, Zürich. At several locations in the underground mall, the light sockets that are recessed into rounded concave concrete surfaces read as tear-drops (Fig. 8.12). The floor structure above the lights is treated just as sensitively by being pared back to elegant tapering ribs with glass-block pavers admitting natural light.

▲ **8.11** Recessed lights in stub columns.

▲ **8.12** Stadelhofen Railway Station, Zürich, Switzerland, Santiago Calatrava, 1990. Integration of structure and artificial lighting.

MAXIMIZING LIGHT

Where requiring high levels of daylight or transparency through the building skin, architects adopt a number of stances towards structural detailing. Maximum daylight implies reducing the silhouette or shadow of structural members. The two most common methods are either to minimize structural member sizes, or to penetrate typically sized members. Transparent structural members are also becoming increasingly popular.

Detailing to minimize structural size

Chapter 7 discusses how the dual architectural qualities of complexity and lightness can arise where structural dimensions are minimized. Simple calculations show that if one tension rod is replaced by two smaller diameter rods with a combined strength equal to the original, the area of the structural silhouette is reduced by approximately 30 per cent. With four rods this reduction in silhouette reaches 50 per cent – the more members, the more light, but also more visual complexity.

At 237 m long, 79 m wide and 28 m high, the vaulted Trade Fair Glass Hall, Leipzig, was the largest single-volume glass building of the twentieth century. The tubular steel exoskeletal structure consists of ten primary trusses that stabilize a grid-shell (Figs 8.13 and 8.14). Triangular in cross-section, the arched trusses are fabricated from relatively small-diameter steel tubes whose varied wall thicknesses reflect the intensity of the structural actions. A resolute strategy to achieve maximum transparency excluded potentially large-scale members from consideration. As Ian Ritchie, project architect, explains:

> *Transparency was a key design objective. We wanted to minimize the structural silhouette, and in fact the total area covered by structure in any*

▲ **8.13** Trade Fair Glass Hall, Leipzig, Germany, Ian Ritchie Architects, 1996. Exterior trusses support the vaulted grid-shell.

▲ **8.14** Trusses and the grid-shell as seen from within the hall.

▲ **8.15** Cité des Sciences et de l'Industrie, Paris, France, Adrien Fainsilber, 1986. Les Serres or conservatories on the main façade.

▲ **8.16** A hierarchy of prestressed cable-beams resist face-loads on the glazed walls.

radial view met our adopted criterion of no more than 15 per cent. (This percentage arrived at by analyzing many of the glass structures we have designed, represents the maximum interference which allows the overall design to have a strong feeling of lightness.)[10]

Even though completed back in 1986, the three glazed conservatories known as Les Serres on the southern façade of the Cité des Sciences et de l'Industrie, Paris, still represent a fine example of structure designed to maximize light (Figs 8.15 and 8.16). Finely detailed horizontal cable-beam girts span 8 m between vertical steel posts to support face-loads acting on the 2 m square glass panels. An enlarged version of the girts transfers horizontal loads from the intermediate vertical posts to each side of the 32 m wide bays. Prestressing the catenary cables to limit the number of structural members acting in compression has enabled this

▲ **8.17** School at Waidhausenstraße, Vienna, Austria, Helmut Richter, 1995. Composite steel walkway beams.

▲ **8.18** Triangular cantilever trusses support the mono-slope glazed roof.

type of detailing to approach the limit of achievable transparency. Glass plays an important structural function by supporting its own weight, hanging from the uppermost tubular steel beams. The transparency of the system is described by one author:

> *The tension trusses sit some distance behind the plane of the glass, and the connections to the glass are so light that they seem almost not to touch the glass. This fact, and the lightness of the tension supporting structure, enhance the feeling of transparency which Fainsilber [the architect] was so keen to achieve. The resulting structure is light and almost ephemeral: the boundary between inside and out is sensitively and lightly defined.[11]*

Although not pushing technological boundaries as hard as at Les Serres, the School at Waidhausenstraße, Vienna, also exemplifies structural detailing that maximizes daylight. A fully glazed circulation spine and two halls, one for assembly and another for sports, link the southern ends of three conventional concrete classroom blocks. Glazed mono-slope roofs rise from the ground floor to enclose the halls and the four-storeyed walkways. Walkway beams of composite construction reduces individual structural member sizes to small I-section beams acting as compression chords and steel rods below them resist the tension component of the bending moments (Fig. 8.17). The assembly hall roof structure cantilevers from a rigid support base to the roof of the classroom blocks. In this case structural lightness is a consequence of generously deep three-dimensional trusses and their relatively fine steel-tube members (Fig. 8.18).

The Carré d'Art, Nîmes, is the final example of detailing that minimizes structural size to maximize light. In order to respect the height of the

▲ **8.19** Carré d'Art, Nîmes, France, Sir Norman Foster and Partners, 1993. Glass stair-treads and the supporting structure in the atrium.

▲ **8.20** Bevelled and set-back beams.

surrounding buildings in its historic city, half the library and contemporary art museum is built below ground. Although the lower three basement floors are not daylit, a six-storey central atrium allows natural light to reach deep inside the building. The problem of channelling light through a space containing the main stairway system is solved by the choice of glass stair-treads (Fig. 8.19). As one reviewer comments: 'The purpose of the glass staircases becomes clear in descent to the lower levels. Daylight transforms what would otherwise have been a gloomy pit into a magical grotto. It is like standing under a waterfall.'[12]

Having successfully brought light down into the atrium, as much light as possible needs to be moved horizontally into the surrounding spaces. In this situation structural detailing enhances this process, more by modifying structural configuration than by reducing structural size. In order to maintain planar concrete ceiling soffits, up-stand beams span between columns. The difference in depth between the beams and slabs creates a space for services under the raised-floors. Where the beams on each storey frame the perimeter of the atrium and also the perimeter walls, they are off-set from the columns in plan, and their sides facing the light are bevelled (Fig. 8.20). This arrangement not only visually slims the floor system, but more importantly, significantly increases the quantity of daylight entering interior spaces.

Penetrations in structural members

Although penetrations through structural members are normally considered aspects of structural detailing and could have been discussed in the previous section of this chapter, such a common and significant response to the need for daylight warrants specific discussion.

Before considering several contemporary examples, two cases of historical interest deserve mention – first, Henri Labrouste's stackroom at the Bibliothèque Nationale, Paris. Giedion describes the highly penetrated floors that are located under a glazed roof:

> *Cast-iron floor plates in a gridiron pattern permit the daylight to penetrate the stacks from top to bottom. Floor plates of this open design seem to have been used first in the engine rooms of steamships ... Nevertheless, observing them in our day, we recognize in the manner in which light penetrates the grillwork of the iron floor the germ of new artistic possibilities.*[13]

Since the popularity of stiletto-heeled shoes, steel-grating floors have limited applications, but as observed at the Carré d'Art, glass flooring is now a well established substitute.

The other notable historical example of light-enhancing structural penetrations occurs in Frank Lloyd Wright's Usonian House, Mount

▲ **8.21**   Schools of Geography and Engineering, Marne-la-Vallée, Paris, France, Chaix & Morel, 1996. A finely perforated web of a steel beam.

▲ **8.22**   Mexican Embassy, Berlin, Germany, González de León and Serrano, 2000. A penetrated circular wall forms part of the atrium.

Vernon. Concrete blocks, L-shaped in plan, are placed and stacked vertically to form U-shaped columns. Both faces of blocks on one side of the U are penetrated and glazed. Objects displayed on glass shelves within the column are illuminated by daylight.[14]

Returning to contemporary examples of structural penetrations maximizing light, the United Airlines Terminal is revisited (see Fig. 7.12). Circular penetrations through beam webs appear to contribute to its well-lit spaces, but given that the lighting designer does not mention them in his lighting strategy, their contribution to the overall lighting levels is probably quite low.[15] At the Schools of Geography and Engineering, Marne-la-Vallée, webs of steel beams are perforated by small diameter holes (Fig. 8.21 and see Fig. 3.49). This method that introduces light through steel sections is likely to be more widely exploited in the future due to its greater subtlety. But as at the United Airlines Terminal, its true value might lie in making the structure *appear* lighter rather than increasing measurably the intensity of daylight.

Windows invariably penetrate concrete structural walls, but smaller and more numerous penetrations may be appropriate when daylight rather than views is sought. A circular atrium sits behind the striking façade of the Mexican Embassy, Berlin, its exterior wall essentially a partial concrete drum (Fig. 8.22 and see Fig. 4.19). 'Capped by a massive

▲ **8.23**   Broadfield House Glass Museum, West Midlands, England, Design Antenna, 1994. Interior of the glass extension.

skylight and punctured on its curved walls by cylindrical portholes, the drum is all about natural light. It evokes the "lightness" of concrete, its dual character, simultaneously delicate and weighty.'[16]

Transparent structure

Secondary and tertiary transparent structural elements in the form of glass window mullions and glass blocks have been used for many years. The Sainsbury Centre for Visual Arts, Norwich, with its full-height glass mullions, was completed in 1977 (see Fig. 5.7). However, only recently have designers' improved knowledge of glass technology led to glass undertaking primary structural roles. Although glass is currently the preferred transparent structural material, no doubt alternative materials will be developed in the future.

A lean-to extension at Broadfield House Glass Museum, West Midlands, relies entirely upon glass structural elements (Fig. 8.23). Laminated glass plates form vertical posts to glazed walls and support glass rafters at glued mortice and tenon joints.[17] Wall and roof glazing provides in-plane bracing resistance.

In the Town Administrative Centre, Saint-Germaine-en-Laye, Paris, in what is considered a world-first, laminated glass columns designed for an axial load of 6 tonnes, support the atrium roof beams (Figs 8.24 and 8.25). The columns, cruciform in section, possess a greenish hue. Any greater degree of transparency would render them almost invisible and therefore hazardous to building users. In this public space the columns delineate circulation and waiting areas from staff workstations. The structure subdivides and orders space without reducing visibility and security significantly. The columns obstruct daylight passing through the glazed walls

▲ **8.24** Town Administrative Centre, Saint-Germaine-en-Laye, Paris, France, Brunet and Saunier, 1995. Glass columns support roof beams.

▲ **8.25** A glass column base detail.

▲ **8.26** Apple Store, New York, USA, Bohlin Cywinski Jackson, 2002. The central glass staircase.

of an internal garden slightly, but such a potentially small shadow effect is of no consequence given the transparent roof. Excessive glare and thermal gain are likely to be far more serious problems.

During the conversion and refurbishment of a 1920s post office into the Apple Store, New York, the architects maximized lightness, transparency and a sense of spaciousness with the provision of a central glass staircase supported by glass load-bearing walls (Fig. 8.26). The space under the stair remains a void except for the glass fins that provide transverse stability and enhance the vertical load-carrying capacity of the glass walls. Below the levels of the stair treads the wall thickness comprises three layers of glass. Two laminated panes support the handrail. The glass landing and stair treads are laminated from four layers of glass. Elegant circular stainless steel fixings connect the glass panes together to achieve a truly transparent structure (Fig. 8.27).

MODIFIER OF LIGHT

Not only does structure act as a source of light and is frequently designed to maximize the quantity of light entering a building, it also modifies the intensity and quantity of light. As well as excluding or blocking light by virtue of its opaqueness, structure also filters and reflects light.

Filtering

Numerous closely spaced and often layered structural members filter light. Where structural layout and density evoke the trees of a forest, as in the Oxford University Museum Courtyard, daylight is experienced as if filtered through a canopy of tree branches (see Fig. 6.39).

▲ **8.27** Stair treads connect to the glass wall.

▲ **8.28** City of Arts and Sciences, Valencia, Spain, Santiago Calatrava, 1998. L'Umbracle with its garden shade-structure.

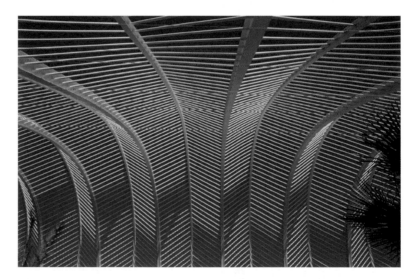

▲ **8.29** Shade-structure arches and ribs.

Roof structure within the Wohlen High School auditorium also plays a strong light-filtering role (see Figs 6.18 and 6.19). Daylight enters the hall through clerestory windows above the interior structure. The closely spaced ribs that radiate from the primary arches act as light filters. A white-stained finish increases the timber's reflectance under both natural and artificial lighting conditions.

Santiago Calatrava's fascination with ribbed structures also finds expression in an exterior structure known as L'Umbracle, in the City of Arts and Sciences precinct, Valencia (Figs 8.28 and 8.29). As well as

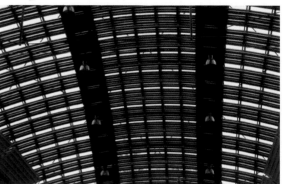

▲ **8.30**　Seed House and Forestry Centre, Marche-en-Femenne, Belgium, Samyn et Associés, 1996. Exterior view.

▲ **8.31**　Shading increases at the splice positions of the transverse arches.

enclosing car parking at ground level, the roof of L'Umbracle functions as a tree-lined garden. An arched and ribbed shade-structure encloses the whole area, and while its ribs are more slender and spaced further apart than those at Wohlen High School, one strongly experiences its light-filtering qualities. Plants growing over the ribs in some areas increase the level of shading.

The interior structure of the Seed House and Forestry Centre, Marche-en-Femenne, also filters light and provides shade (Figs 8.30 and 8.31). Bentwood arches that span the building width support the completely glazed ovoid form. Longitudinal arches provide stability in the orthogonal direction. The combination of closely spaced arches and 100 mm wide members leads to significant areas of shade, especially where the timbers are lap-spliced. Strong striped patterns of sunlight and shadow enliven the interior spaces.

Reflecting

Structural members screen direct sunlight but also provide surfaces off which it may reflect and then diffuse into surrounding space. The deep atrium beams of Louis Khan's Philip Exeter Library, Exeter, already mentioned in this chapter, exemplify this interaction between structure and light even though some commentators have queried whether the beams achieve sufficiently high light levels at the ground floor level in the atrium. They point to the small quantity of direct light admitted through the partially shaded clerestory windows, and the low reflectivity of the grey concrete beams.

Roof beams in the Mönchengladbach Museum receive significantly more direct light and, also due to their lighter colour, play a more influential

▲ **8.33**   Business School, Öhringen, Germany, Günter Behnisch & Partner, 1993. A primary beam with the skylight above and the roof below.

▲ **8.32**   Mönchengladbach Museum, Germany, Hans Hollein, 1982. Beams screen and reflect light into the gallery below.

role in screening sunlight and reflecting it into the gallery (Fig. 8.32). A similar approach is taken in the Business School gymnasium, Öhringen (Fig. 8.33). The white-stained glue-laminated beams that span the width of the hall reflect rather than screen light. North-facing translucent glazing slopes from a lowered ceiling and up and over the beams that project above the roof line. Their raised location with respect to the roof eliminates any possibility of their screening direct sunlight at the end of a day when the sun's rays are almost horizontal, but the reflectivity of the beams increases the effective width of the glazed roof areas and therefore the intensity of illumination within the gymnasium.

Surfaces of structural members also provide opportunities for reflecting artificial light. The Vancouver Public Library, Vancouver, is typical of many buildings where a comfortable level of background lighting is reflected from suspended floor soffits (Fig. 8.34 and see Fig. 3.1). Uplights illuminate the vaulted concrete slabs whose shallow coved surfaces are well suited to achieving appropriate levels of indirect and diffuse light.

Fabric structures are well known for their ability to reflect and diffuse light. Their conventional white coloured and shiny surfaces (dark fabrics are prone to severe solar overheating) guarantee a high degree of reflectivity which responds well to uplighting. The ability of the fabric to diffuse light is best experienced on a sunny day. Fabric translucency that

▲ **8.34**   Library Square, Vancouver, Canada, Moshe Safdie and Associates Inc., 1995. An uplit vaulted ceiling.

▲ **8.35**   Mound Stand, Lord's Cricket Ground, London, England, Michael Hopkins and Partners, 1987. Underside of the fabric roof.

varies according to thickness and the type of fabric provides relatively low-intensity light that is even and soft. The Mound Stand, London, is a typical example (Fig. 8.35). Although the PVC-coated polyester fabric primarily provides shade, a pleasant quality of diffuse light filtering through the canopy is also noticeable.

MODIFIED BY LIGHT

Although structure often controls light – its intensity and quality – the relationship between structure and light is not entirely dominated by structure. For light not only reveals structure, but also modifies one's perceptions of it. Millet explains how in two churches of very different character, one Bavarian rococo and the other contemporary North American, glare from relatively intense and well-controlled daylight dematerializes their structures and has structural members perceived as luminous lines.[18]

Dematerialization occurs where an area of structure that is illuminated far more intensely than the surrounding ambient light levels seems to disappear or at least loses its sharpness of definition in the bright haze. For example, the lengths of columns that pass through a window display-case in the Timber Showroom, Hergatz, are so brightly illuminated when exposed to strong sunlight that they merge into the glary background (Fig. 8.36 and see Fig. 5.6). The columns therefore read as not being grounded. They appear to stop above the window opening, thereby increasing the visual complexity and interest of the building. It is unlikely that this visual effect, which may go unnoticed on a dull day, was intended by the designers whose focus of attention would have been the provision of adequate fenestration to display the company's products. A similar

▲ **8.36**   Timber Showroom, Hergatz, Germany, Baumschläger-Eberle, 1995. Glare dematerializes the base of the portal legs. They appear to terminate at the top of the display window.

effect is observed at Saint Benedict Chapel, Sumvtg (see Fig. 6.4). Where interior posts pass in front of the clerestory, glare from their surfaces reduces their clarity and the starkness of their silhouettes against the sky, and intensifies the perception of the roof floating.

Intentional dematerialization of structure by light characterizes the work of the contemporary architect Juan Navarro Baldweg. According to one reviewer, Baldweg develops the theme of light and structure in a completely new way:

> Here light prevails over shade, homogeneity over contrast. A diffuse and even light that descends from above can be obtained by removing every last trace of shadow: thus the roof is transformed into a combined system of V-shaped girders and skylights, becoming a luminous mechanism ... Just as the girders are given a triangular cross-section to eliminate every remaining cone of shade, so to the pillars acquire a triangular section, so as to obtain, through the play of light, an effect of dematerialization of the wall.[19]

The combination of structure and artificial lighting can also be used to considerable aesthetic effect in both exterior and interior situations. For example, the ground floor exterior columns of **88 Wood Street**, London are singled out for illumination by down-lighting, that at night, transforms them into cylinders of light (see Fig. 4.4). Illumination of the Tokyo International Forum exposed interior roof structure produces a

▲ **8.37**   Mönchengladbach Museum, Germany, Hans Hollein, 1982. Geometrical patterns of light subvert the sense of inhabiting an orthogonal structural grid.

considerably more dramatic effect: 'At night, light reflecting off the surface of the roof truss ribs transforms the structure into a monolithic floating light source illuminating the glass hall and assuring the visual presence of the building in the Tokyo skyline.'[20]

In the final example where structure appears to be modified by light, light disrupts the perception of an orthogonal structural layout. At the Mönchengladbach Museum, an approximately 6 m square column-grid is imposed upon the irregular-shaped main gallery. Rather than visually reinforcing the grid geometry by means of beams or other elements, lines of artificial lighting achieve the opposite effect. Lengths of fluorescent tubes that are surface-mounted on the plain ceiling create polygonal patterns of light that break down one's perception of inhabiting a grid (Fig. 8.37). Drawn to the light, the eye follows the lines of brightness. Their patterning provides a welcome visual alternative to that of the orthogonal structural layout.

SUMMARY

Structure and light are both indispensable and interdependent elements of architecture. While structure may control light – its locations of entry into a building and its quantity and quality, the need for daylight inevitably determines structural form and detailing. Although during the design process structural decisions may be subservient to those concerning light, once built, roles reverse and structure controls light.

After acknowledging Louis Kahn's innovative integration of structure and light, the chapter explores how open structure can act as a source for light to enter a building. Structural form, members and even structural connections all participate in this role. Readers are also reminded of how structural layout often delineates the shapes of transparent areas in the exterior skins of buildings.

The integration of structure and both transparency and the ingress of daylight is achieved by a variety of approaches. These include detailing structure with more smaller rather than fewer larger members, penetrating solid structural members to 'lighten' them, and using glass or translucent structural members.

Since sunlight is unwelcome in certain spaces, structure plays light-modifying roles. Structure filters and reflects, producing even and diffuse qualities of light. Finally, examples illustrate how light modifies one's perception of structure. Light dematerializes structure, has structure read primarily as a source of light, and subverts awareness of structural rationality.

REFERENCES AND NOTES

1 Meiss, P. van (1990). *Elements of Architecture: From Form to Place*. Presses Polytechniques Romandes, p. 121.
2 Millet, M. S. (1996). *Light Revealing Architecture*. Van Nostrand Reinhold, p. 60.
3 Tyng, A. (1984). *Beginnings: Louis I. Kahn's Philosophy of Architecture*. John Wiley & Sons, p. 145.
4 Tyng (1984), p. 146.
5 Comments by Louis Kahn compiled in Johnson, N. E. (1975). *Light is the Theme: Louis I. Kahn and the Kimbell Art Museum*. Kimbell Art Foundation, p. 21.
6 Dimond, R. and Wang, W. (eds) (1995). *On Continuity*. 9H Publications, p. 188.
7 Ron W. (ed.) (2002). *CASE: Toyo Ito Sendai Mediatheque*. Prestel.
8 For a pictorial explanation of the construction sequence see Branch, M. A. (1991). Internationally styled. *Progressive Architecture*, 72 (4), pp. 87–93.
9 Balmond, C. (2002). *informal*. Prestel, p. 316.
10 Ritchie, I. (1997). *The Biggest Glass Palace in the World*. Ellipsis London Ltd, p. 34.
11 Brown, A. (2000). *The Engineer's Contribution to Contemporary Architecture: Peter Rice*. Thomas Telford Ltd, p. 73.
12 Davies, C. (1993). Norman Foster. *Architecture*, Sept., pp. 106–9.
13 Giedion, S. (1978). *Space, Time and Architecture*, 5th edn. Harvard University Press, p. 224.
14 Millet (1996), p. 63.

15 Shemitz, S. R. (1987). Lighting the way. *Architectural Record*, 175 (13), pp. 148–155.
16 Bussel, A. (2001). Great expectations. *Interior Design*, 72 (7), pp. 297–301.
17 For construction details refer to Dawson, S. (1995) Glass as skin and structure. *The Architects' Journal*, 210 (10), pp. 32–4.
18 Millet (1996), p. 66.
19 Zardini, M. (1998). Light and structure in Juan Navarro Baldweg's work. *Lotus International 98*, p. 56–9.
20 Toy, M. (ed.) (1997). Light in architecture. *Architectural Design Profile 126*. John Wiley & Sons, p. 43.

9

REPRESENTATION
AND SYMBOLISM

INTRODUCTION

This chapter explores how exposed structure enriches architecture when structural forms and details contribute meaning by virtue of their representational and symbolic qualities. Structural representation is understood as structure typifying a physical object, like a tree or a crane, while symbolic structure recalls an idea, a quality or a condition. Like beauty, representation and symbolism lie in the eye of the beholder.

Both representational and symbolic structure encompass different degrees of explicitness. While some examples of representation are almost universally recognized, others are not. The situation is even more pronounced in the case of symbolism. When discerning symbolic meaning in architecture, as in any object, one brings his or her whole life to bear upon it. One's imagination, upbringing, education, life experiences, sense of well-being and professional expertise all influence how meaning in architecture in general, and in exposed structure in particular, is perceived. It is little wonder then that many symbolic readings are completely unimagined by designers.

Architect Sverre Fehn illustrates the deeply personal nature of human response to structural representation and symbolism. He sensitively imagines an individual's response to an exposed structural member, a column:

> In the church the fisherman enters his pew. From his seat he recognizes that the column has the same dimensions as his mast. Through this recognition he feels secure. He sits by his column, a form also acknowledged by the gentle touch of his fingers. On the open sea, the tree was a symbol he trusted, as it brought him safely home. The same representation assists him now in turning his thoughts towards prayer. Within his spirit the sea is calm. In his search for the stars, the column offers him a personal dialogue.[1]

This passage exemplifies structure, in this case a column, playing both representational and symbolic roles. Although both roles may be being played simultaneously when a structure is read, the following sections discuss each role separately.

REPRESENTATION

Examples of structural representation can be divided into two unevenly sized groups. In the far larger group, sources of representation include objects and processes found in the natural world. Artifacts, that comprise the smaller group, also become sources of design inspiration and invite attempts at representation.

The limited number of examples that this chapter describes is but a fraction of all possible structural representations. Plant forms that recall the shapes of well-developed trees are by far the most common. Only in the Eden Project (see Fig. 3.5), whose hexagonal structured biomes are scaled-up versions of bumblebee eye structures, is structure based on natural microscopic or molecular forms. This is not to deny the potential for other sources of inspiration from the natural world. Forms from plants, the worlds of animals, birds, insects and marine life, and forms from naturally occurring solids like metals and crystals are all latent sources of representation.[2]

Natural world

In the context of discussing the designs of young Finnish architects, Antoniades suggests that 'one may classify as a uniquely Finnish obsession, the introduction of tree-form elements into architecture'.[3] He illustrates numerous examples where tree and forest have inspired and generated structural form in recent architecture, and he includes some conceptual explorations of trees as generators of high-rise building structures. However, while many examples of arboreal columns are to be found in Finland, articulation of column as tree occurs in many, if not most countries.[4]

Of all natural forms, trees and forests are by far the most likely to be represented structurally, and their popularity among architects is reflected in the case-studies that follow. After exploring a number of different structures that manifest tree forms, several buildings are considered where the structure is more likely to be read as forest, and then the chapter moves on to examples that exhibit the geological process of erosion and various anthropomorphic and zoomorphic features.

Structural trees dominate the main façade at the Palais de Justice, Melun (Fig. 9.1). An entrance canopy that extends across the building frontage rests upon six tree-like columns. Apart from the small fins radiating from the perimeter of the trunk bases to deter intending graffiti artists, these columns are literal steel replicas of trees. Like real trees, they

▲ **9.1** Palais de Justice, Melun, France, Jourda & Perraudin architectes, 1998. A tree-supported canopy on the main façade.

▲ **9.2** Science Museum, Valencia, Spain, Santiago Calatrava, 1998. Two of the giant structural trees with galleries behind.

possess trunks and forked branches. Even twigs exist, located immediately underneath the canopy. Only the leaves are missing! Such explicit representation raises the question how do the trees relate to the building's interior? Once inside does one promenade along a tree-lined avenue? Unfortunately, in this building no connection exists between its exterior and interior architecture – the trees are little more than an architectural gesture, albeit one that is rather grand.

In an equally literal example of representation, steel tree-columns transform the interior of the Stuttgart Airport Terminal (see Fig. 3.43). Structural twigs penetrate the wall glazing at first floor level to support an entrance canopy. Linking interior and exterior architecture they hint at the interior grove of trees within. Again stick-like and leafless, the branches indicate either an endless winter or death, but their complexity and intricacy more than compensate for their starkness, and they arouse interest and admiration.

'Trees' also become the primary interior elements of the Science Museum, Valencia. They visually separate the huge entry and exhibit hall from the three levels of galleries behind (Fig. 9.2). Although the main branches spread out in just two dimensions, the form of the five white concrete elements is quite unambiguous.

Whereas in the previous two examples the trunks and branches are formed by linear members, the branches of the structural trees at the

In the final three examples where the structural representation of the tree is less explicit, large numbers of columns evoke the notion of the forest or the plantation. For instance, one identifies more with the concept of the forest than with the tree where: 'Rows of rough hewn columns of ancient pine march through the cavernous space in regimented, arboreal splendor', at the Mont-Cenis Academy, Herne (see Fig. 3.27).[6] While each column is little more than a de-barked log, one faces only numerous tree-trunks, and a canopy without branches. The forest, rather than the tree, is again communicated in the Baumschulenweg Crematorium, Berlin (see Fig. 2.13). Its plain cylindrical columns are devoid of branches. Although such regular columns on their own could hardly be considered to represent trees, their sheer numbers and their collective 'random' placement evokes a forest. In another variation on the forest theme, one is reminded of the multitudinous leaning canopy posts under the Melbourne Exhibition Centre verandah (see Fig. 4.13). They can be read alternatively as river-bank reeds or plantation wind-blown saplings.

Whereas the previous buildings in this section exemplify structure representing either trees or forest, the structure at the rear of the Outdoor Activities Centre, Portsmouth, suggests a natural process – erosion. Although the Centre's exposed timber construction and metal fasteners deny the hostility of its coastal location only several metres from the sea shore, the western side of the building, facing inland yet subject to prevailing winds, incorporates masonry and concrete construction (Fig. 9.9). When approaching the building from the car park, one passes two bays of externally buttressed masonry walls that 'break down' and eventually become a colonnade of free-standing buttresses closer to the main entrance of the Centre. Given the disappearance of sections of the wall and of the full wall panels along most of the length of the building, a geological process like erosion springs to mind, even without overt signs such as crumbling bricks and jagged or worn surfaces. This example of representation is certainly not explicit, and in fact nothing in the architect's account of the building supports this reading.

Anthropomorphic and zoomorphic sources are also represented by structural form and detailing. Chapter 7 comments upon the elegantly detailed metal castings at the Lyons School of Architecture (see Fig. 7.30). Their ribs not only express the flow of internal forces but are also expressive of the visual characteristics of human fingers. Also, consider the pier-plinth 'feet' in the Stadelhofen Railway Station underground mall, Zürich (see Fig. 7.52), and the similarly shaped base-plates under the entrance canopy to Wohlen High School (Figs 9.10 and 9.11). In another design by Santiago Calatrava, his fascination with bones and

▲ **9.9** Outdoor Activities Centre, Portsmouth, England, Hampshire County Architects, 1995. Where the building is approached from the car park in the background, the partial or full disappearance of the wall panels suggests a process like erosion.

▲ **9.10** Wohlen High School entry canopy, Switzerland, Santiago Calatrava, 1988. Ribs cantilever from the main arch.

▲ **9.12** Terminal building, Railway Station at Satolas Airport, Lyons, France, Santiago Calatrava, 1994. The central arched-spine and its supporting buttresses (during construction).

▲ **9.11** Feet-like base-plates to the window mullions behind the canopy.

skeletons finds expression in the arched spine-like truss of steel vertebrae that spans the length of the main terminal building at Satolas Airport, Lyons. Thrusts from the arch are transferred into the foundations by zoomorphic shaped external buttresses (Fig. 9.12). Around the

▲ **9.13**   Armenian School Library, Los Angeles, USA, StudioWorks Architects, 2003. The 'ark' is elevated above the school playground.

perimeter of the Palazetto dello Sport, Rome, inclined exterior struts that resist compression loads from its ribbed-shell roof resemble athletes with arms extended, stretching their calf muscles by pushing against a wall (see Fig. 3.3).

Artifacts

Architectural books and journals contain many examples of structural representation originating other than from the natural world – areas such as aeronautical, nautical and automotive engineering, and industrial and historic structures, are but a few sources.

Several buildings where structure represents different types of artifacts have already been encountered. Drawing upon nautical imagery, ribbed timber construction defines the curved surfaces at the European Institute of Health and Medical Sciences, Guilford (see Fig. 3.28), and under the Némausus Apartments, Nîmes, uniformly-distributed slender columns create the impression of the building floating. Shear walls that read as rudders, given their location at the rear of the 'ship' and their rudder-like elevational profile, provide longitudinal stability for the ground floor (see Fig. 5.13).

▲ **9.14**   The main columns align with the keel and are flanked by stabilizing posts.

The nautical theme surfaces again at the Armenian School Library, Los Angeles, a new addition to an already cramped site. Raised one storey above the ground, four large red elliptically clad columns and some slender steel tubes are the library's only footprint (Figs 9.13 and 9.14). The ark, as it is known, is intended to recall the account of the biblical Noah's ark which is important in Armenian culture, as well as to symbolize aspects of Armenian immigration to countries like the USA. Its clear ark-like form, with walls elliptically shaped in plan, a rounded hull and an expressed keel, is held aloft by two different structural elements. The large columns placed under the centrally located keel are assisted by secondary props whose main task is to ensure transverse stability. Even then, the ark appears quite precariously balanced. Although the props are symmetrically and regularly placed, because the outer props support the intersections of the faceted planes that form the ellipse, and due to their inclination to the vertical, they read as randomly placed. This strengthens the idea of make-shift propping stabilizing a grounded craft. In spite of the absence of interior transverse ribs and the deployment of internal pairs of columns on the same centres as the large columns beneath, the shape of the interior space and its entirely unfinished plywood wall linings more than adequately continue the narrative begun outside.

The roof structure of the Atlântico Pavilion, Lisbon, similarly responds to a maritime theme. Glue-laminated arched and trussed frames span up to 115 m to enclose the arena and its concrete seating structure (Figs 9.15 and 9.16):

> Built for Expo '98, a world's fair that commemorated the 500th anniversary of explorer Vasco da Gama's voyage from Portugal to India . . . the shape of the roof resembles the inverted hull of the carabelas, the type of ship used by de Gama; the arena's wood ceiling and heavy wood support ribs pay homage to the construction of the carabelas.[7]

The youth club in Möglingen, Stuttgart, exemplifies more literal structural representation. After consulting with the teenage user-group, the

▲ **9.15** Atlântico Pavilion, Lisbon, Portugal, Skidmore Owings & Merrill PLC, 1998. The sleek pavilion roof is in the background.

▲ **9.16** Timber trussed-arches over-sail the seating.

▲ **9.17** Youth Club, Möglingen, Stuttgart, Germany, Peter Hübner, 1996. Building exterior.

architect has created a work of narrative architecture that incorporates two seemingly disparate elements – a space-craft and mud. The overall form, and especially the exterior structure, bears strong resemblance to a space-craft, while the theme of mud is realized by the non-structural earthen walls (Figs 9.17 and 9.18). Although the steel ribbed-dome roof and its perimeter open-truss utilize a High-Tech vocabulary, the realistically detailed 'retractable legs' speak loudly of space-age technology. The source of inspiration behind their detailing, especially their struts and rods that articulate the compression and tension connections to the perimeter truss, and the circular landing pads at their bases, is unmistakable.

Wohlen High School is revisited again to discuss the fourth and final set-piece in the school designed by Santiago Calatrava – the library roof. From his preliminary sketches it is clear that the structural form of the roof draws upon the shape of an open soft-covered book or the out-stretched wings of a bird flying (Fig. 9.19).[8] It consists of a folded and curved concrete shell whose weight is supported by a tubular steel column reinforced by ribs whose curved shapes give rise to its spindle-shaped profile. Horizontal stainless-steel rods located around the perimeter of the roof in several locations stabilize it by tying it back to structural walls. Daylight washes down the walls through gaps between them and the roof.

Although the roof form resembles the pages of an open book or the wings of a bird, the enfolding presence of its curved concrete surfaces immediately above the mezzanine reading galleries provides a strong sense of enclosure and protection. These emotions, evoked by the combination of the structural form and the perimeter lighting, reinforce

▲ **9.18** A primary structural roof support displaying space-age detailing.

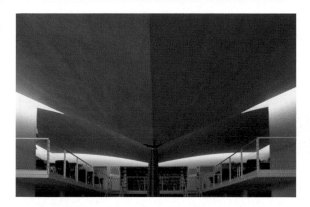

▲ **9.19** Wohlen High School library roof, Switzerland, Santiago Calatrava, 1988. A central column supports the roof shell which 'shelters' the mezzanine galleries to the rear.

▲ **9.20** Church of the Autostrada, Florence, Italy, Giovanni Michelucci, 1968. The church as seen from the motorway.

▲ **9.21** Dramatic interior structure with the main altar to the left facing the rows of seats. (Courtesy F. Amadei.)

▲ **9.22** Details of the concrete structure.

a reading derived from the natural world – that of the wings of a bird sheltering her offspring.

The Church of the Autostrada, Florence, contains the final example of structure representing an object from the human world. Situated on the outskirts of Florence adjacent to the motorway, the church commemorates those workers who lost their lives building Italy's modern motorway system. Both architect and reviewers agree that the church's tent-like form simultaneously acknowledges the nomadic life of the ancient Israelites and the travelling public driving past the church (Fig. 9.20). However, opinions pertaining to the interpretation of its dramatic interior structure remain divided.

I refer to the amazing array of irregular struts that support the roof and also differentiate the sanctuary from the nave, frame the main altar, and screen off a passage-way (Figs 9.21 and 9.22). One reviewer suggests that the structural forms allude to: 'the calcified bones of a skeleton, and to desiccated stems'.[9] While a preliminary cross-sectional sketch by the architect suggests tree-like supports, the architect, Giovanni Michelucci, denied any intention of naturalistic representation. Instead, he referred to his desire to introduce fantasy, variety and surprise into his architecture, and acknowledged how forms inspired by trees contribute to that process.[10] He insists that no particular representation or symbolism was intended, other than allowing 'fantastic' structural shapes to invite a variety of readings. Perhaps the church's programme as a monument to the human cost of civil engineering construction suggests another reading? To me, this unconventional and intriguing structure, both in terms of its form and its exquisite irregularly modelled surfaces, reads as an abstraction of construction scaffolding, props and temporary bracing, and other construction equipment like derricks or cranes.

With this building fresh in our minds, a building whose structure defies categorization, that can be interpreted in many ways, and possesses a palpable and tantalizing sense of both representation and symbolism, examples where structures play more obvious symbolic roles are now considered.

SYMBOLISM

The practice of people imbuing structure with meaning is commonplace both outside and inside the architectural community. Several examples that are drawn from quite different sources, including two from the world of vernacular architecture, illustrate this activity.

Kenneth Frampton includes an analysis of an Algerian Berber house by the sociologist Pierre Bourdieu:

> In addition to all this, at the center of the dividing wall, between 'the house of human beings' stands the main pillar, supporting the governing beam and all the framework of the house. Now this governing beam which connects the gables and spreads the protection of the male part of the house to the female part . . . is identified explicitly with the master of the house, whilst the main pillar on which it rests, which is the trunk of a forked tree . . . is identified with the wife . . . and their interlocking represents the act of physical union.[11]

A very different and religious symbolic meaning is attached to the exposed interior structure of the Rangiatea Church, Otaki, which was, until recently, New Zealand's oldest church: 'The ridge-pole, fashioned from a single tree, symbolizes the new faith and a belief in only one god. The ridge-pole is supported by three pillars symbolizing the Christian Trinity.'[12]

Exposed interior roof structure seems particularly amenable to symbolic interpretation. Lance LaVine writes of house ridge beams:

> As a cultural artifact, the ridge beam is the center of the roof that covers human habitation. It is this center that preserves the human mind and spirit, as well as the needs of the human body, and thus this unique building element has gained a special place in the collective human memory of place or, perhaps more importantly, of being in places. The ridge of a house not only centers its roof structure but in so doing becomes a symbol for a centered existence within that form. It is a unique place in a dwelling that has come to secure the human psyche as it gathers the live and dead loads of the roof rafters that it helps to support.[13]

While still on the subject of roof structure, and considering the meaning embodied in a vaulted roof, LaVine continues: 'A flat surface may extend indefinitely without ever protecting an inhabitant at its edges. To be covered is to have something that wraps around human beings . . . The vault of the house covers inhabitants as blankets cover their bed as the sky covers the earth.'[14]

Angus Macdonald also acknowledges the symbolic role of structure in architecture. In his categorization of possible relationships between structure and architecture he includes a category, 'structure symbolized'. Here 'structure is emphasized visually and constitutes an essential element of the architectural vocabulary . . . the "structure symbolized" approach has been employed almost exclusively as a means of expressing the idea of technical progress . . .'.[15] He explains that symbolic intent can encompass issues other than celebrating technology and explores the implications of structure symbolizing an ideal – like sustainability.

An implicit assumption that structure plays symbolic roles in architecture underlies this book. For example, Chapter 2 discusses how the unique detailing of the BRIT School columns symbolizes notions of innovation and creativity, and how the sombre and giant columns of the Baumschulenweg Crematorium are likely to be a source of strength for those who mourn (see Figs 2.1 and 2.13). At the Kunsthal, Rotterdam, exposed structural detailing that questions conventional attitudes to aesthetics, expresses the ethos of a museum of modern art (see Figs 7.10 and 7.11), while the elegance of detailing at Bracken House, London, conveys a sense of quality and prestige (see Fig. 7.39).

As already seen, structure plays a wide range of symbolic roles. While some symbolic readings are unintended by architects, in other cases architecture is enriched quite explicitly by exploiting the symbolic potential of structure, as exemplified in three buildings designed by Daniel Libeskind.

▲ 9.23 Jewish Museum, Berlin, Germany, Daniel Libeskind, 1998. Structural members pass chaotically above the main stairs.

▲ 9.24 Felix Nussbaum Museum, Osnabrück, Germany, Daniel Libeskind, 1998. Dysfunctional concrete beams in the Nussbaum Corridor.

In the Jewish Museum, Berlin, structural members play important symbolic roles. They reinforce the symbolism inherent in the whole project, but that is especially evident in the plans and elevations of the fractured building. Concrete struts-cum-beams pass chaotically across the main stairwell leading to the exhibition galleries (Fig. 9.23). Orientated at different angles with varied cross-sectional shapes and dimensions, these members symbolize the historical dislocations and horrors experienced by the German Jews. The convincing materiality and scale of the struts suggest structurally important roles, even though their chaotic configuration contradicts such a possibility. Although the struts prop the external wall to some degree, their primary role is symbolic. They enhance the architectural concept. This ominous and unexpected structure is laden with meaning.

Structure also contributes to the narrative architecture of the Felix Nussbaum Museum, Osnabrück. It helps recount the tragic story of the Jewish painter after whom the museum is named.[16] Structure, together with the building plan, building exterior, and the architectural details, speaks of violence, isolation and disorientation. For example, structural walls and a ceiling slab enclose the high and dimly lit Nussbaum Corridor that leads visitors to the main galleries. The harshness of the grey concrete, the lack of any detailing to relieve the plainness of the elongated space, and the dysfunctional concrete beams passing over it intensify the sense of loneliness and horror faced by Nussbaum as he entered a period of exile (Fig. 9.24). Elsewhere, structure evokes equally poignant emotions. Some structural walls possess sharp and angled edges, and structural members passing through windows and across overhead light-slots read unmistakably as bars of prison cells (Fig. 9.25). Together with other architectural elements, as well as the museum collection itself, structure recounts Nussbaum's life in a chilling and jarring manner.

Fragmentation as a design concept is also incorporated into the Imperial War Museum-North, Manchester. Its architectural form reflects a view of the world shattered into three fragments, depicting the devastating effect of war. These fragments, or 'shards', brought together to form the main museum volumes, represent conflict on land, water and in the air. The main museum space is accommodated in the Earth Shard while the Water Shard contains a restaurant and café. The Air Shard takes the form of an irregularly shaped and slightly canted tower which houses a viewing platform at roof level.

Open to the elements, the Air Shard is essentially a soaring 30 m high void – except for its interior structure (Fig. 9.26). All museum visitors

▲ **9.25** Beams passing across the light-slot read as the bars of prison cells.

▲ **9.26** Imperial War Museum-North, Manchester, England, Studio Daniel Libeskind, 2002. Structural members dominate the Air Shard volume.

enter the tower at ground level and pass through it towards the museum proper. While rain and wind pass through the generous gaps between its aluminum cladding battens and accentuate the bleakness of the space, the greater assault upon the senses arises from the structure that fills the volume. Steel tubes fly through the space, seemingly at all angles. They form a multi-member spatial framework that appears chaotic. The structural members appear to be mapping the three-dimensional trajectories of war planes through the sky.

Libeskind's works have influenced the design of Federation Square, Melbourne. The fragmentation of its façade surfaces and their supporting structures is recognized as symbolizing a number of aspects of Australia's culture – the individuality of Australia's eight states and territories, its ethnic diversity and its relationship with the indigenous people. Behind the fractural patterned glazing mullions and cladding panels, structural form intensifies the idea of fracture through its 'random' three-dimensional frameworks that support some roofs and exterior walls.

From within and outside two of the main public spaces, the Atrium and the interior BMW Edge amphitheatre, structural forms appear totally chaotic, verging on possible spatial versions of Pick-up Sticks (Figs 9.27 and 9.28). Load paths are impossible to trace. There are no recognizable structural systems or patterns, such as frames, arches or trusses, and no geometrical predictability. Most structural rules and traditions are broken as horizontal and vertical members are avoided and eccentric connections between members become commonplace. This is an example of structural anarchy. When lit at night the structure appears as a tangled thicket of bare tree branches.

As well as symbolizing some of the realities of Australia's national life, most of which are in fact universally applicable, other fundamental issues as well are raised by the welded and rigidly connected steel hollow-section frameworks. Given one's inability to categorize them and understand their workings, one is forced to accept that their structural performance is beyond understanding and trust in the expertise of those few structural engineers responsible for their digital structural analyses and designs. This structure forces its viewers to accept the unknown and live beyond their prior experiences. It also acknowledges the reality of the irrational and the unpredictable, that is, the environment much of life is lived in.

By comparison with the explicit structural symbolism in the previous four projects, any intended meaning in the exposed structure of the Industrial Park Office Building, Völkermarkt, is far less obvious. Even though the nature of its exposed structure is far more flamboyant than

▲ **9.27** Federation Square, Melbourne, Australia, Lab Architectural Studio and Bate Smart Partners, 2002. The tangled structure of the Atrium roof.

that of previous examples, it solicits different interpretations and creates a refreshing degree of mystery in the same manner as the Church of the Autostrada, Florence, discussed in the previous section.

Providing office accommodation, the building is a gateway for a light industrial park dedicated to start-up or emerging business enterprises. It consists of three elements; a narrow concrete walled-structure housing stairs and a lift that connects to the main concrete frame rising five storeys above a ground level podium. The frame supports the third and the most interesting element, a curved cantilevered steel structure (Figs 9.29 and 9.30).

After commenting on a previous design by the same architect that was interpreted as a criticism of the capitalist system, Peter Davey writes:

> It is difficult to see how this building is a criticism of the system . . . perhaps it is a claw against the sky, or possibly a tattered crow's feather with its filaments flying. But the main impression is of welcome and thrust, the swirling curve of a powerful living, glossy bird's wing: a signal of strength, virility, generosity and hope.[17]

Another interpretation might focus on the different characteristics of the frame and the cantilever. Perhaps the heavy, orthogonal and certainly conventional frame epitomizes the capitalistic system, while the light and flexible cantilevered area represents the new enterprises that

▲ **9.28** A perimeter walkway though the wall structure of the BMW Edge ampitheatre.

▲ **9.29**   Industrial Park Office Building, Völkermarkt, Carinthia, Austria, Günther Domenig, 1996. The framed block supporting the cantilever and the lift and stair tower behind.

are twisting, turning and climbing in an effort to break free from it and its constraining rigidity? Then again, perhaps the curvature of the cantilever in plan is merely responding to the geometry of the road which bends around the base of the building?

SUMMARY

After acknowledging how representation and symbolism ranges from the literal to the ambiguous, this chapter illustrates the individualistic and personal nature of how meaning in structure is discerned. It then continues with examples of representation that draw upon the natural world for their inspiration. Trees, followed by forest are the most common sources, but anthropomorphic and zoomorphic forms are also included. Representation based upon human artifacts is less common but ship, boat, space-craft and book forms are also represented by structure. The section concludes with the representational and symbolic ambiguity of Michelucci's remarkable Church of the Autostrada.

Structural symbolism, inherent in the concept of reading structure, is implicit throughout this book. Before recalling numerous examples from previous chapters, several other authors demonstrate just how widespread is the practice of imbuing structure with meaning. Three buildings by Daniel Libeskind illustrate structure playing explicit symbolic roles, and the chapter concludes by considering a final building where any definitive meaning remains delightfully elusive.

▲ **9.30**   Steelwork of the braced cantilever structure.

REFERENCES AND NOTES

1   Fehn, S. (1983). *The Thought of Construction*. Per Olaf Fjeld and Rizzoli International Publications, p. 46.

2   Pearce, P. (1978). *Structure in Nature is a Strategy for Design*. The MIT Press, ch. 2.

3   Antoniades, A. C. (1992). *Epic Space: Towards the Roots of Western Architecture*. Van Nostrand Reinhold, p. 256.

4   See, for example, Cook, J. (1996). *Seeking Structure from Nature*. Birkhäuser.

5   For an explanation of the geometric complexity of the construction refer to Burry, M. (1992). Gaudí: the making of the Sagrada Familia. *Architects' Journal*, 195 (13), pp. 22–51.

6   Kugel, C. (1999). Green academy. *Architectural Review*, 206 (1232), pp. 51–5.

7   Bussel, A. (2000). *SOM Evolutions: Recent Work of Skidmore, Owings & Merrill*. Birkhäuser, pp. 60–5.

8   Blaser, W. (ed.) (1989). *Santiago Calatrava: Engineering Architecture*. Birkhäuser, p. 35.

9   Dal Co, F. (1992). Giovanni Michelucchi: a life one century long. *Perspecta 27, The Yale Architectural Journal*. Rizzoli International Publications, pp. 99–115.

10 de Alba, R. H. and Organschi, A. W. (1992). A conversation with Giovanni Michelucci. *Perspecta 27, The Yale Architectural Journal*. Rizzoli International Publications, pp. 116–39.

11 Quoted in Frampton, K. (1995). *Studies in Tectonic Culture: The Poetics of Construction in Nineteenth and Twentieth Century Architecture*. Massachusetts Institute of Technology, p. 14.

12 Tumatatoa, P. (1990). Churches illustrate impact of new faith. *New Zealand Historic Places*, 29, 40–4. Unfortunately the original church was destroyed by fire several years ago. A replica was opened in 2003.

13 LaVine, L. (2001). *Mechanics and Meaning in Architecture*. University of Minnesota Press, p. 125.

14 LaVine (2001), p. 151.

15 Macdonald, A. J. (1997). *Structural Design for Architecture*. Architectural Press, p. 30.

16 After going into exile and evading capture for many years, the young Nussbaum and his partner were killed in a Nazi concentration camp in 1944.

17 Davey, P. (1996). Spirit of Ecstasy. *Architectural Review*, 199, pp. 54–9.

10   CONCLUSIONS

INTRODUCTION

The fact that most of the previous chapters in this book focus on specific areas or aspects of architecture suggests a need to summarize the main themes emerging from this study. This final chapter then, draws together the three principal strands that weave through each of the preceding chapters.

Before tying off these threads, it is necessary to recall briefly the main purpose of the book – to analyse structure architecturally rather than structurally. That is, to observe and read structure through the eyes of an architect and a building user, rather than adopting the narrower and more technically focused eye of a structural engineer. Structure, therefore, is viewed as a mainstream architectural element rather than as a secondary element originating from the often self-contained 'Structures' discipline of schools of architecture. Drawing upon examples from more than one hundred and seventy built works, this book presents a comprehensive analysis and categorization of the roles that structure plays in contemporary architecture.

As such, the book functions as a source book for designers. Although careful not to advocate the *necessity* of incorporating exposed structure into a building, it presents a vision of structure as a potentially exciting architectural element, and one that should always be integral with the design concept. Precedents in the book will trigger designers' imaginations and suggest ways for them to further develop their individual ideas. The book can also be used as a mirror against which designs may be assessed. It may, for example, help designers to reflect on the architectural qualities of their own interior surfaces and spaces, and to ponder as to whether they have exploited structure fully enough. Does structure contribute explicitly to their architecture and help realize and communicate their design concepts?

In most cases, structure contributes to architecture aesthetically – stimulating one's senses and engaging emotions and minds. Given its dominant visual presence, structure impacts most significantly upon our sense of sight. However, in some situations the surface smoothness of a structural member, or the manner in which it has been hand-crafted might encourage us to physically connect with it through touch. Structure is rarely experienced through smell, although the fragrance of freshly milled and erected timbers might be savoured. And, apart from an awareness of the acoustic screening or the reverberation properties of concrete and masonry structural walls, structure rarely impinges upon one's sense of hearing.

TRANSFORMATIVE POWER OF STRUCTURE

Throughout this book many examples illustrate how structure transforms otherwise bland surfaces and spaces, both exterior and interior. By virtue of its composition-making and space-making qualities, structure introduces visual interest and character. Surfaces take on a degree of interest and 'spaces become places'. Additional architectural enrichment flows from structure's interaction with light, or by offering meaning to viewers through its representational and symbolic qualities.

Structure is not a neutral architectural element. It influences the space around it, and its very presence invites architectural analysis or readings. This book encourages architects to develop a strong proactive stance towards structure, rather than resigning themselves to perceiving structure as purely utilitarian. Architects should allow their design ideas to drive the structural design. They should make the most of structure as an architectural element, beginning with its form and layout, and further enliven their designs through structural detailing. The architectural success of any structure should be assessed by the extent to which it realizes a design concept, or in other words, enriches a design.

This perception of structure creates opportunities rather than constraints. Such a positive attitude releases structure from the shackles of conventional practice and its two masters of constructability and economy, and frees it to play more substantial functional and aesthetic roles in architecture. Just as a structural overlay upon an architectural plan or section bestows an additional sense of constructional reality to an otherwise diagrammatic representation, exposed structure transforms surfaces, spaces and viewers' experiences of built architecture.

STRUCTURAL DIVERSITY

There are a surprisingly large number of modes by which structure enriches architecture – the most important being to assist the realization of the design concept. In order to achieve this goal, exposed structure will be prominent in one or more of the areas of architecture discussed in the previous chapters, such as in intensifying or contrasting with architectural form, or modifying the visual appearance of the exterior or interior of a building. Structure, in all likelihood, will also be carefully integrated with building function, for example, by articulating spaces for circulation. It will often play a role in introducing daylight into a space and modifying some of the qualities of light. Success with the big picture is achieved where structure relates to all aspects of the design, down to the smallest structural detail.

Within each area of architecture the contribution of structure can take one of many possible forms. Consider the large number of examples illustrating different structural details or ways that structure interacts with daylight. Diversity also abounds given the number of structural systems available. For example, designers can chose between three-dimensional surface-structures such as at the Saint Massimiliano Church, Varese (see Fig. 6.10), spatial frameworks like those at the Portland Building, Portsmouth (see Fig. 6.16), and essentially two-dimensional systems like structural walls. As well as a choice of structural materiality, designers also have a huge diversity of structural scale at their disposal – members that vary in size from 10 mm diameter cables to trusses over 5 m deep.

Given the huge number of structural possibilities, designers have considerable freedom of choice. This sets the scene for innovative and creative structural designs. But because of the goal that structure should actively reinforce the design concept, each structural decision requires to be thought through strategically. Future technological advances in structural materials and in analysis and design techniques will inevitably continue to increase both the diversity of structural options and their architectural implications.

The impacts of structure upon those who experience it are also diverse. One structure, exuding a sense of tranquility, soothes emotions. Another sets nerves on edge. A raw and inhospitable structure contrasts with one that welcomes and expresses a sense of protection. As outlined in Chapter 9 especially, structures are also capable of conveying an enormous range of meanings to passers-by and building occupants.

IMPLICATIONS FOR THE ARCHITECTURAL AND STRUCTURAL ENGINEERING PROFESSIONS

With its emphasis upon structure as an architectural element this book encourages a broad, creative and critical stance towards structure. It presents an alternative approach to some current practice where the most expedient structural engineering solution is adopted unless its impact upon the architectural concept is considered to be disastrous. For structure's potential as an enlivening architectural element to be realized, collaboration between the architect and the structural engineer needs to be extensive and intensive.

Architects need to take an active role in all stages of structural design, working with the structural engineer in order to achieve mutually acceptable outcomes. Beginning with preliminary structural layouts through to detailed design at working drawing stage, both groups of professionals together need to wrestle with the various options. Structure is owned by both professions and it must satisfy simultaneously the requirements of both – load-bearing as well as architectural expression.

This book will help bridge the gap between both professions. Through it, architects will become more aware of how structure can enrich their designs. This will lead them to request structural engineers to explore how less conventional structural responses might integrate better with their design concepts. Through such a process, structural engineers will grow in their awareness that the systems and members they design and detail for strength and stiffness possess considerable architectural value and represent far more to architects and the general public than just a means of load-bearing. Architecturally enriching structure is likely to require greater analytical and design skills. It challenges designers' reliance upon a formulaic approach to structural design where the most construction-friendly and economic design is adopted. Finally, an increased appreciation of how exposed structure plays important architectural roles will increase a sense of pride among structural engineers and strengthen the sense partnership between the two professions.

A further implication of the fact that structure is of vital importance to both professions suggests the need for on-going reflection upon how 'Structures', that subject within schools of architecture curricula, is taught. In most schools, engineers teach the subject within the architectural technologies section of the programme. Little mention is made of structure's architectural roles. By increasing the level of integration of 'Structures' with architectural design, students' interest in structures and their awareness of its relevance to their designs will be enhanced – along with the quality of their architecture.

INDEX OF BUILDINGS AND REFERENCES

The page number(s) on which the buildings feature in this book are given in bold.

125 Alban Gate, London, **98–9**
Gough, P. (1993). Three Urban Projects, Architect Terry Farrell. Blueprint Extra 09, Wordsearch.

88 Wood Street, London, **54–5, 185**
Powell, K. (2000). Capital gain. *Architects' Journal*, 211:1, 22–31.

Apple Store, SoHo, **180**
Barreneche, R. A. (2002). Apple Store, New York City, SoHo. *Architectural Record*, 10.02, 156–61.

Armenian School Library, Los Angeles, **196–7**
Jarmusch, A. (2003). Mental gymnastics. *Architecture*, 92 (9), 60–5.

Atlântico Pavilion, Lisbon, **197**
Spier, S. (1998). Expansive arena. *Architectural Review*, 204 (1217), 31–3.

Attic conversion, Vienna, **154**
Stein, K. (1989). Over the edge. *Architectural Record*, 177 (9), 82–91.

Beehive, Culver City, **150**
Hutt, D. (2002). In Culver City, California, Eric Owen Moss builds the BEEHIVE – a playfully sculptural structure and a creative workplace abuzz with activity. *Architectural Record*, 08:02, 130–5.

Bibliothèque Sainte-Geneviève, Paris, **162–3**
Gargiani, R. (1997). Ornament and construction in the library of Ste-Geneviève, Paris, 1839–1850. *Casabella*, 61 (645), 60–73.

Bilbao Metro, **94–5**
Anon (1997). Norman Foster: Bilbao Metro, Bilbao, Spain. *GA document*, 52, 98–101.

Bracken House, London, **74–5, 151–2, 201**
Winter, J. (1992). Inside job: Bracken House. *Architects' Journal*, 195 (21), 26–37.

BRIT School, Croydon, **7–13, 137, 201**
Taggart, B., Foley, M. and Barbrook, R. (1992). College designed to change. *Architects' Journal*, 196 (14), Oct. 7, 37–49.

Broadfield House Glass Museum, West Midlands, **179**
Dawson, S. (1995). Glass as skin and structure. *Architects' Journal*, 201 (10), 32–4.

Building Industry School, Hamm, **109**
Hesser, M. and HHS Planer + Architekten (1996). Schulungsgebäude in Holzbauweise. *Baumeister-Themenmagazin*, Okt., 38–41.

Burrell Gallery, Glasgow, **172**
Glancey, J. (1984). The Burrell: art and nature. *Architectural Review*, 175 (1044), 28–37.

Business School, Öhringen, **72–3, 183**
Blundell-Jones, P. (1995). Behnisch in Ohringen. *Architectural Review*, 197 (1178), 33–7.

California College of the Arts, San Francisco, **99**
Woodbridge, S. B. (2003). Solar Studies – a rehabilitated 1950s building in San Francisco offers lessons in light and air. *Architecture*, 92 (4), 82–5.

Canary Wharf Underground Station, London, **95**
Hardingham, S. (2000). Canary Wharf station, Jubilee Line extension, London. *Domus*, 825, 50–4.

Canopy structure, World Exhibition Centre, Hanover, **59–60**
Dawson, L. (2000). Expo-Dach. *Architectural Review*, 208 (1243), 46–9.

Carpentry School, Murau, **143–4, 170**
Blundell-Jones, P. (1994). Wood works. *Architectural Review*, 194 (1163), 52–7.

Carré d'Art, Nîmes, **176–7**
Davies, C. (1993). Carré culturel. *Architectural Review*, 194 (1157), 18–31.

Casa del Fascio, Como, **34**
Blundell-Jones, P. (2002). *Modern Architecture Through Case Studies.* Architectural Press.

Cathédrale Nôtre Dame de la Treille, Lille, **63–4**
Kutterer, M. (1999). West façade of Lille Cathedral. *Detail*, 39 (6), 962.

Centraal Beheer Office Building, Apeldoorn, **92–3, 112**
Colquhoun, A. (1974). Centraal Beheer. *Architecture plus*, 2 (5), 48–55.

Dulles International Airport, **27, 58**
Freeman, A. (1980). The world's most beautiful airport? *Architecture: AIA Journal*, 69 (13), 46–51.

Eden Project, Cornwall, **24–5**
Allen, I. (2001). A taste of Eden. *Architects' Journal*, 213 (7), 30–9.

Education Centre, Newport, **89–90**
Roach, P., Phillips, N., Hannay, P. *et al.* (1994). A hand-made link to the Iron Age. *Architects' Journal*, 200 (1), 29–39.

Eighteen Turns, Serpentine Gallery 2001, London, **39–40**
Young, E. (2001). Now you see it . . . *RIBA Journal*, 108 (9), 68–70.

European Institute of Health and Medical Sciences, Guildford, **35–6, 196**
O'Looney, B. (2000). Nicholas Grimshaw & Partners: European Institute of Health, University of Surrey, Guildford. *Domus*, 64–71.

Exchange House, London, **20, 41**
Harriman, M. S. (1990). London Bridge: engineering, structural steel. *Architecture: AIA Journal*, 79 (9), 109–12.

Exhibition Centre, Melbourne, **60, 194**
Slessor, C. (1997). On the wing. *Architectural Review*, 201 (1201), 57–8.

FABRICA (Benetton Communication Research Centre), Treviso, **139–40**
Pearson, C. (2001). Tadao Ando sculpts the Italian landscape and engages in a dialogue with history at the new Fabrica complex in Treviso. *Architectural Record*, 189 (1), 80–7.

Faculty of Journalism, Vicens and Ramos, Pamplona, **33**
Anon. (2001). Faculty building in Pamplona. *Detail*, 41 (1), 70–3.

Faculty of Law Building, Cambridge, **156, 160**
Best, A. (1996). Legal precedent. *Architectural Review*, 199 (1189), 34–42.

FDA Laboratory, Irvine, **107**
Sullivan, C. C. (2004). Flexible and crisis-ready, a new laboratory building is a living metaphor for its owner, the FDA. *Architecture*, 93 (3), 48–56.

Federation Square, Melbourne, **203–4**
Jencks, C. (2003). The undulating Federation Square, designed by Lab Architecture, mirrors the city and country through dissonance and harmony. *Architectural Record*, 06.03, 108–17.

Felix Nussbaum Museum, Osnabrück, **202**
Ingersoll, R. (1998). Libeskind builds. *Architecture: AIA Journal*, 87 (9), 110–17.

Ferry Terminal and office building, Hamburg, **141**
Dawson, L. (1993). Eye catcher on the Elbe. *Architectural Review*, 193 (1159), 45–9.

Financial Times printing works, London, **82–3**
Winter, J. (1988). Glass wall in Blackwall. *Architectural Review*, 184 (1101), 42–50.

Fisher Center, Bard College, Annadale-on-Hudson, **142–3**
Stephens, S. (2003). Frank Gehry merges intuitive and rational forms at Bard College to create an evocative performing arts center. *Architectural Record*, 07.03, 106–17.

Fitzwilliam College Chapel, Cambridge, **71–2, 119–20**
Blundell-Jones, P. (1992). Holy vessel. *Architects' Journal*, 196 (1), 24–37.

Fleet Place House, London, **42**
Bussel, A. (2000). SOM evolutions: Recent Work of Skidmore, Owings & Merrill, Birkhäuser.

Frankfurt Messenhalle 3, **84**
Pearman, H. (2000). *Equilibrium*. Phaidon.

Getty Center, Los Angeles, **61**
Brawne, M. (1998). The Getty Center: Richard Meier & Partners. Phaidon.

Glasgow School of Art, **149**
Harbison, R. (1989). Glasgow School of Art. *Architects' Journal*, 189 (24), 41–59.

Grand Louvre, Paris, **133–4, 154–5**

Grande Arche, Paris, **31, 133**
Davey, P. (1989). La Defense. *Architectural Review*, 186 (1110), 44–53.

Great Court, British Museum, London, **49–50, 111–12**
Pople, N. (2001). Caught in the web. *RIBA Journal*, 108 (2), 36–44.

Great Glasshouse, Carmarthenshire, **30**
Melhuish, C. (2000). Green, green glass of home. *Architects' Journal*, 212 (9), 30–9.

Güell Colony Crypt, Barcelona, **107–8**
Martinell, C. (1975). *Gaudi: His Life, His Theories, His Work*. MIT Press.

Guggenheim Museum, Bilbao, **141–2**
Lootsma, B. (1998). A Gehry for Bilbao: the new Guggenheim Museum. *Archis*, 1, 16–25.

Hall 26, Trade Fair, Hanover, **27, 169**
  Dawson, L. (1997). Wave motion. *Architectural Review*, 201 (1201), 42–6.

Hamburg Airport: Terminal 3, **95–6**
  Binney, M. (1999). *Airport Builders*. Academy Editions.

Hamburg Museum Courtyard Canopy, **162–4**
  Lampugnani, V. (1990). Glazed cover to the courtyard of the Museum of Hamburg History. *Domus,* 719, 66–73.

Hazel Wood School, Southampton, **139**
  Dawson, S. (1991). Elegant classroom canopy. *Architects' Journal focus,* June, 15–19.

Hong Kong and Shanghai Bank, Hong Kong, **51–3, 98**
  Doubilet, S. and Fisher, T. (1986). The Hong Kong Bank; architects: Foster Associates. *Progressive Architecture*, 63 (3), 67–109.

Hotel de las Artes, Barcelona, **64–5**
  Iyengar, H., Zils, J. and Sinn, R. (1993). Steel exoskeleton defines architecture. *Civil Engineering*, 63 (8), 42–6.

Hôtel du Département, Marseilles, **44–5, 79**
  Welsh, J. (1994). Willing and able. *RIBA Journal*, 101 (4), 36–47.

Imperial War Museum-North, Manchester, **202–3**
  Russell, J. (2002). With the Imperial War Museum North, Daniel Libeskind builds his case for a major museum destination on a budget. *Architectural Record*, 190 (10), 124–31.

Industrial Park Office Building, Völkermarkt, **203–4**
  Davey, P. (1996). Spirit of Ecstasy. *Architectural Review*, 199 (1190), 54–9.

Institut du Monde Arabe, Paris, **157–8**
  Boles, D. (1987). Modernism in the city. *Progressive Architecture*, 68 (7), 72–80.

Jewish Museum, Berlin, **202**
  Spens, M. (1999). Berlin Phoenix. *Architectural Review*, 205 (1226), 40–6.

JFK Airport: Terminal 4, **89**
  Amelar, A. (2002). JFK Terminal 4 Queens, New York. *Architectural Record*, 01.02, 114–17.

Jussieu University, Paris, **145–6**
  Herve, M. (1990). *Guide to Modern Architecture in Paris*. Syros-Alternatives.

Kew Recreation Centre, Melbourne, **170**
  Hyatt, P. (1989). Undercover. *Steel Profile*, 28, 26–30.

Reichstag cupola, Berlin, **28–9, 49**
Davey, P. (1999). Democracy in Berlin. *Architectural Review*, 206 (1229), 34–47.

Research Centre, Seibersdof, **97**
Kugel, C. (1996). Hive of industry. *Architectural Review*, 199 (1190), 45–9.

S. Giorgio Maggiore, Venice, **70–1**
Wundram, M., Pape, T. and Marton, P. (1989). *Andrea Palladio, 1508–1580: Architect between the Renaissance and Baroque*. Benedikt Taschen.

Sagrada Familia, Barcelona, **193**
Burry, M. (1993). *Expiatory Church of the Sagrada Familia: Antoni Gaudí*. Phaidon.

Sainsbury Centre for Visual Arts, Norwich, **84, 179**
Stephens, S. (1979). Modernism reconstituted. *Progressive Architecture*, 60 (2), 49–58.

Saint Benedict Chapel, Sumvtg, **105–7, 133, 185**
Steinmann, M. (1989). Peter e Annalisa Zumthor: Cappella a Sogn Benedetg, Svizzera. *Domus*, 710, 44–53.

Saint Massimiliano Kolbe church, Varese, **109–10**
Servadio, L. (1999). The cosmic sphere rising out of the water: a new church for Varese. *Architettura*, 45 (527), 508–14.

San Cataldo Cemetery, Modena, **31–2, 94**
Freiman, Z. (1991). The architect of the city. *Progressive Architecture*, 72 (2), 50–63.

San Francisco International Airport, **169–70**
Ward, J. (2001). Air Traffic Control. *Architecture*, 90 (6), 74–80.

Sant Jordi Sports Hall, Barcelona, **171**
Branch, M. (1991). Internationally styled. *Progressive Architecture*, 72 (4), 78–83.

Säntispark Health and Leisure Centre, St Gallen, **38–9**
Anon. (1987). Freiziet-und Einkaufszentrum Säntispark bei St Gallen. *Schweizer Baublatt*, 3, 10pp.

Satolas Airport: Railway Station, **140, 173–4**
Slessor, C. (1993). Big bird on a wire. *Architectural Review*, 193 (1159), 61–6.

Satolas Airport: Railway Terminal building, **195–6**
Rogers, L. (1994). Lyons made. *RIBA Journal*, 101 (8), 32–7.

Stazione Termini, Rome, **43**
Mulazzani, M. (2001). Stazione Termini, Roma. *Casabella,* 65 (695), 88–101.

Stealth Building, Culver City, **47–8**
Giovannini, J. (2001). Constant change. *Architecture*, 90 (11), 98–107.

Stellingen Ice Skating Rink and Velodrome, **25–6, 169, 171**
ASW (1997). Dach fur eine Sportarena in Stellingen. *Baumeister*, 94 (2), 38–40.

Stratford Regional Station, **147**
Russell, J. S. (1999). Setting the pace for innovative transit design, Chris Wilkinson advances his station on the English architectural scene. *Architectural Record*, 07.99, 114–8.

Stuttgart Airport Terminal, **42, 191**
Von Gerkan, M. (1993). Von Gerkan, Marg & Partners. Academy Editions.

Suhr office building, **134–5**
Steinmann, M. (1986). Ein Haus wie ein UFO. *Archithese*, 16 (2), 45–54.

TGV Station, Lille, **42–4**
Davey, P. (1996). The boot and the lace maker. *Architectural Review,* 199 (1189), 72–3.

Thermal Baths, Vals, **86**
Ryan, R. (1997). Primal therapy. *Architectural Review*, 202 (1206), 42–8.

Timber Showroom, Hergatz, **83–4, 184**
Valdes, O. (1996). Showroom and warehouse, Hergatz, Germany. *Domus*, 782, 32–7.

Tobius Grau KG office, Rellingen, **36–7, 135–6**
Dawson, L. (2000). Industrial revolution. *Architectural Review*, 207 (1235), 52–5.

Toskana Thermal Pools, Bad Sulza, **83**
Roskam, F. *et al.* (2002). Sportbauten. *Deutsche Bauzeitschrift*, 50 (2), 34–88.

Town Administrative Centre, Saint-Germaine-en-Laye, **179–80**
Behling, S. and S. (eds) (1999). *Glass: Structure and Technology in Architecture*. Prestel.

Trade Fair Glass Hall, Leipzig, **174–5**
Pepchinski, M. (1996). Crystal palace for reborn trade centre. *Architectural Record*, 184 (11), 80–9.

Wohlen High School, entrance foyer roof, **104–5**
Peters, T. F. (1989). Crossing boundaries. *Progressive Architecture*, 4 (89), 8–103.

Yerba Buena Lofts, San Francisco, **54**
Pearson, C. A. (2002). Stanley Saitowitz tests the market for high Modernism with his Yerba Buena lofts in San Fransisco's South of Market district. *Architectural Record*, 08.02, 117–21.

Youth Club, Möglingen, **198–9**
Blundell-Jones, P. (1996). Space craft. *Architectural Review*, 200 (1195), 44–7.

INDEX